Short Stories from Vedas with Student Takeaways

11 Vedic lessons
for Every Student Success

Vedas & Upanishads

for Children

AVINASH AGARWAL

DISHA™
Publication Inc

DISHA Publication Inc.

A-23 FIEE Complex, Okhla Phase II
New Delhi-110020
Tel: 49842349/ 49842350

Typeset By
DISHA DTP Team

DISHA™
Publication Inc

Write To Us At
feedback_disha@aiets.co.in

Preface

In this fast-paced and ever-changing world, it becomes crucial to instil in our children a sense of deep-rooted values, a broader perspective of life, and an appreciation for the wisdom of our ancestors. The Vedas and Upanishads provide a treasure trove of knowledge and wisdom, guiding individuals towards a path of self-discovery, ethical living, and spiritual growth.

This book aims to make these profound teachings accessible and engaging to young minds. The book presents key concepts, stories, and lessons from the Vedas and Upanishads in a simplified and age-appropriate manner, ensuring that children can grasp the essence of these ancient texts. Through captivating stories, inspiring anecdotes, and thought-provoking discussions, this book offers a glimpse into the vast universe of Vedic and Upanishadic wisdom. It encourages children to explore fundamental questions about life, the self, the universe, and the interconnectedness of all beings.

Moreover, this book aspires to ignite curiosity, stimulate critical thinking, and foster a sense of wonder and awe in young readers. It encourages them to contemplate deeper truths and to develop a broad and inclusive worldview, embracing diversity, compassion, and respect for all.

I express my heartfelt gratitude to the ancient sages who gifted humanity with these timeless teachings and to the parents, teachers, and guardians who play a vital role in nurturing the intellectual and spiritual development of our children. May this book be a valuable resource for them on their path to wisdom.

In writing this book, my objective is to share the deep knowledge and wisdom of Vedas and Upanishads with students and young readers all over the world. My first book 'Bhagvada Gita' was a step in this direction. I am truly humbled by the response that I received for that book. I sincerely hope that this book, too, meets all its objectives and leaves an everlasting impact on the impressionable minds of the readers.

With warm regards

(Avinash Agarwal)
www.avinashagarwal.in
E-mail : avinash@aiets.co.in
avinash_studycoach
Avinash Agarwal

Table of Contents

01

Where It All Begins!

As a child, whenever I saw my grandmother praying to God every day, without any break, I often wondered who was she praying to? Why couldn't I see God or the one who created this world. I was quite attached to my grandmother. When I had just turned 10, I lost her. The pain was unbearable to me. I could not understand what to do or how to handle that situation. I was unaware of what was happening around me. I kept on crying for days and asked my parents innumerable questions – how could I bring my grandmother back? Why has she left me? so on and so forth. Also, I became anxious if I was also going to die one day, what would happen to me after that. My parents had no answers to any of my questions. They simply consoled me and tried to distract my mind. However, blame it on my curious nature or whatever, all my questions kept bothering me. They disturbed me every now and then. I tried to figure out things on my own but could not, I guess I was too young that time.

Today, as a mature and grown-up being, I realize that at that stage, it was actually very difficult for my parents to make me understand the theories of this universe, the mystery of life and death and many such related things. Also, there is a possibility that they themselves did not have the answers. Today, I believe that if someone genuinely wishes to quench this kind of thirst, the only way for him/her is to seek the help of our scriptures and texts, which provide us knowledge and help us delve into the mysteries of this world. If you are also among those few who are curious to know what our Vedic texts state about God and his wonderful creation, you are at the right place. I am confident that the next few pages will definitely make you more aware of yourself and your surroundings; you will turn out to be a better person, and automatically a better student. You will learn some valuable lessons from our scriptures, which would help you grow, succeed and live a peaceful, contented life.

To understand our scriptures, we have to look at the foundational works of Hinduism, which are categorised into **Shruti** and **Smriti**. In Sanskrit, the literal meaning of the word '**Shruti**' is '**that which is heard**'. It refers to the texts that are believed to have been revealed by the Gods themselves to ancient sages and were passed verbally from one generation to the next. It was through the regular recitation of these sacred texts that this transmission was made possible. Thus, Shruti texts are considered to be the voice of God. They are believed to be divine. Since they are heard or revealed, *shruti* texts do not have a human composer. Not only do *shruti* texts have no human composer, but they also don't change from age to age.

Hinduism believes that there are four yugas—*satya* or *kritayuga*, *tretayuga, dvaparayuga* and *kali yuga*. The *shruti* texts remain the same, regardless of which yuga we are in. In *satyayuga or kritayuga*, everyone was naturally virtuous. You didn't need special rules to ensure good conduct. However, as one progressed down the ladder, from *treta* to *dvapara* and thence to *kali yuga*, people became prone to evil. You needed a template for *sadachara* and once that got codified, it became a *smriti text*. The primary *Shruti* texts are the Vedas. They mainly constitute hymns devoted to forces of nature. They contain in them oceans of knowledge. Every stanza, every line, every word of Vedas hold significant meaning. The popular 'Gayatri Mantra' has also come to us from the Vedas. We often recite this mantra but do we really know what it means or what are the benefits of chanting this mantra?

The Gayatri Mantra is a universal prayer enshrined in the Vedas. It is actually a salutation to the sun or Savitri. Chanting this mantra is a significant rituals among Hindus. It is a belief that chanting Gayatri Mantra firmly establishes our mind and fills our life with joy and happiness. The mantra goes like this:

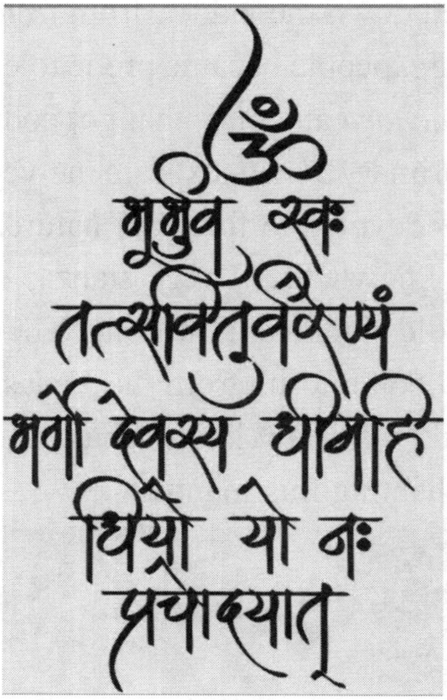

This means - O thou existence Absolute, Creator of the three dimensions, we contemplate upon thy divine light. May He stimulate our intellect and bestow upon us true knowledge.

In simple words, when we chant this mantra, we say- **O Divine Mother, our hearts are filled with darkness. Please take away this darkness and promote illumination within us.**

'**Smriti**', on the other hand refers to 'something which is remembered'. It is a discussion of the texts that were composed based on the teachings and principles of the *Shruti* texts. These texts are actually a guide to religious and moral duties, social customs, and practical applications of the principles found in the Shruti texts. The Smriti category of Vedic literature includes the majority of Hindu texts such as **Dharmashastra** texts (like Manu Samhita), the **Nitishastra** texts (like Panchatantra), **Itihasa** (Ramayana, Mahabharata) and the **Puranas**.

While less authoritative than Shruti, Smriti texts were crucial for explaining and applying Vedic knowledge in social and ethical contexts, making them more accessible and adaptable.

So, to put it briefly, Shruti texts or the Vedas are considered as the highest authority in Hinduism as they are believed to be divine knowledge given by Gods themselves, while Smriti texts provide guidance on how to incorporate and assimilate the teachings and principles found in the Shruti texts in our everyday lives.

The History & Origin of Vedas

Long before the planet Mars was discovered, Indian sages had uttered the fact that there was a red planet out there in the solar system. From snippets of atomic movements to exact descriptions of planets, from medicine to music and from mathematics to art, these million-year old scriptures unfold a treasure house of ancient knowledge. Tales depict that Vedas embody the revelations of enlightened seers called *Maharishis*, and that they jingle with the highest spiritual truth that the human mind is capable of. It is said that the majority of words emanated in the form of ancient hymns through the literary tongue of these scriptures, stamps an eternal truth. Yet, despite it all, what remains obscured is the 'Problem of Origin of Vedas'.

Indian Scriptures

- **Shruti**
  - **Vedas**
    - Rigved
    - Yajurved
    - Samved
    - Atharvved
  - **Section of Vedas**
    - Samhita
    - Brahman
    - Aranyak
    - Upnishads
  - **Vedang**
    - Vyakaran
    - Jyotish
    - Nirukt
    - Shiksha
    - Chand
    - Kalp Sutras
  - **Upved**
    - Ayurved
    - Gandharvaved
    - Dhanurved
    - Sthaptyaved
- **Smriti**
  - **Dharma Shastra**
    - Manu Smriti
    - Yagyavalka Smriti
    - Narad Smriti
    - Vishnu Smriti
    - Parashar Smriti
  - **Puran**
    - **Mahapuran (18)**
      - Brahmapuran
      - Vishnupuran
      - Shivpuran
      - Agnipuran
      - Matsyapuran
    - **Uppuran (18)**
      - Sanatkumar
      - Narshihpuran
      - Durvasapuran
  - **Itihas**
    - Ramayan
    - Mahabharat
  - **Darshan**
    - Nyay
    - Vaisheshika
    - Sankhya
    - Yog
    - Mimansha
    - Vedant
  - **Gita**

Where did Vedas spring from? Who is their author? How did they come into existence? Well, umpteen schools of philosophy have vividly discussed the theme of the origin of Vedas, still and all, the answer reveals itself only through a blurry lens.

Among the many schools of philosophy, there are three main schools which have offered their commentary on the origination of Vedic literature. These three schools are Mimansa, Nyaya and Vaisesika.

Mimamsa states that Vedas are authorless and *svatah-pramana* (self-evident means of knowledge). As per this school of thought, Vedas are characterized as *Apaurusheya*, **that is, not of a man or of divine origin.**

On the other side, schools of Nyaya and Vaisesika support the idea that Vedas were created by ancient *rishis,* those who had realized the manifest form of God.

Some Other commentary on the Origin of Vedas are as follows:

Origin of Vedas according to Puranic literature

According to Puranic literature, the Vedas were written about a system of ceremonial rites addressed to the personified Powers of Nature or *Panchamahabhutas,* namely, fire, air, earth, water and space. These texts stressed that Vedas were created by different deities – Rigveda by the deity of Fire, Yajurveda by the deity of air and Samaveda by the Sun deity.

Origin of Vedas according to the Bhagvad Gita

Adding a mystical dimension to the theory of Vedic origin, the Bhagvad Gita states that all of the Vedas have been created from the word Om. The sages first heard this sound of Om (ॐ), which is also the reason why the Vedas acquired the name "*Shrutis*". Vedas, in the form of a word (*shabda*) or divine speech (para vani) originated from absolute ether in the subconscious mind (chidaksh), from the letters *a* (अ), *u* (उ), *m* (म) and subtle sound respectively. Sages, for years and years, realized this knowledge and passed it down from generation to generation through the word of mouth.

It was only during the time of culmination of *Mahabharata Yuddha* that Sage Vyasa observed that the verses (*shlokas*) of the Vedas were scattered in different lineages (*gotras*). It was only then that he sorted out all the verses and the script for Vedas was compiled for the first time. He divided the Vedas into four parts in order to preserve the knowledge in its pristine purity.

The collection of hymns and verses was first scripted in the Rig Veda in books called as *mandalas*. The verses that could be sung came under the category of Samaveda. The section of the Veda focused on performing sacrificial fires (yajnya), was included in the Yajurveda. The Atharvaveda was created by compiling the mantras useful in performing magic and helping in worldly life.

Origin of Vedas according to Atharvaveda

Atharvaveda states that Rig, Yajur, Sama and Atharva (referring to the four Vedas) originated from the ultimate *Ishwara* or

God. Atharva is like the mouth of that Ishwara, Samaveda is like the hair on the skin, Yajurveda is akin to the heart and Rigveda is the Prana or source.

What Shankaracharya said about the Origin of Vedas?

Shankaracharya writes in commentary on Gita that Vedas are never really created or destroyed. They simply get illuminated and de-illuminated over and over again, yet always residing in one formless essence.

So, finally, where did vedas come from?

To summarise various commentaries and theories; the Vedas were put together, over centuries, by several anonymous rishis or sages. However, Vyasa, which means 'compiler' is believed to be the one who collected the vast and sprawling body of literature we know today as the Vedas. He, then, classified all the different, random bits of it, decided which portions went together and compiled them into chunks. He then divided those chunks into four separate Vedas. For accomplishing this mammoth task in an efficient and organized manner, he was, appropriately so, given the title 'VedaVyasa' – the compiler of the Vedas.

The Vedas are written in an ancient form of Sanskrit, the language which is considered the mother of many modern languages. Studying the Vedas helps students develop a deeper understanding of the Sanskrit language, which in turn enhances their grasp of other Indian languages and improves their linguistic abilities.

When Vyasa compiled the Vedas, he categorised Vedas into four types. In chronological order, they are the Rig Veda, the Yajur Veda, the Sama Veda and the Atharva Veda. Together they are called as 'Chaturveda'. The Chaturvedas are divided into two categories: Karma Kanda and Jnana Kanda based on their respective content.

Karma Kanda refers to that part of the vedas which deals with ceremonial rites and rituals. Jnana Kanda refers to that part of the vedas which deals with the ways through which one can attain liberation and knowledge. We will study about each of these Vedas in length but before that, let's understand that these four Vedas are further classified into four layers or divisions:

The Samhitas: The word 'Samhita' is a Sanskrit word, which in literal terms means 'put together, joined or collection', thus it is a collection of texts or verses. This is the oldest and the simplest part of each Veda. The Samhita is the core of Vedas. It is the actual collection of mantras, hymns and prayers. The Vedic Samhitas were chanted during ceremonies and rituals.

The Brahmanas: It consists of the commentaries and interpretations of the mantras. It is also called as the Karma Kanda of the Vedas. This section lists rituals, ceremonies and actions, which when performed, lead to self-fulfilment. There are minute details on how a particular ritual was performed. However, this part of the Vedas is written in a language, which is not easy to understand.

The Aranyakas: This part of the Vedas discusses and explains the philosophy behind the ritualistic ceremonies and sacrifice. Known as **"forest treatises"**, these texts were studied by sages in solitude and acted as a bridge between ritualistic Brahmanas and philosophical Upanishads.

The Upanishads: The Upanishads are the **philosophical culmination** of the Vedas, focusing on metaphysics, the nature of reality, the concept of Brahman (universal soul), and Atman (individual soul). These texts emphasize knowledge through introspection and spiritual realization. Here, the philosophical message of the Vedas is discussed in the form of conversation between the teacher and the student. Thus, the Upanishads are actually a part of the Vedas. In fact, they are the concluding portions of the Vedas or the end of the Vedas. The teaching based on them is called **Vedanta.** (**वेद + अंत = वेदांत**)

Vedangas, Upavedas and Sad-darshana

Vedangas

To facilitate the correct understanding, preservation, and application of the Vedas, a specialized body of auxiliary knowledge developed over time. These disciplines are collectively known as the Vedangas (literally meaning "limbs of the Vedas"), signifying that they are essential to support and uphold the Vedas. The Vedangas helped scholars interpret Vedic texts with precision, enabling both ritualistic accuracy and philosophical clarity.

There are six Vedangas, each addressing a specific dimension of Vedic learning, including language, ritual, pronunciation, and time calculation.

1. **Shiksha (Phonetics):** Shiksha deals with the correct pronunciation and intonation of Vedic mantras. It includes rules for sound, pitch, and articulation to preserve the oral tradition of the Vedas.

2. **Kalpa (Ritual Instructions):** Kalpa provides systematic rules for performing rituals, including sacrificial ceremonies and domestic rites. It includes ŚrautaSūtras, GrhyaSūtras, and Dharma Sūtras.

3. **Vyakarana (Grammar):** Vyakarana is the study of Sanskrit grammar. It ensures linguistic accuracy in Vedic texts. Panini's Ashtadhyayi is the most prominent work in this field.

4. **Nirukta (Etymology):** Nirukta focuses on the explanation of difficult Vedic words. Yaska's Nirukta is a key text, providing meanings and interpretations to clarify obscure terms.

5. **Chhandas (Prosody):** Chhandas is the study of poetic meter. It ensures that Vedic hymns maintain their rhythmic structure and are chanted correctly according to their meter.

6. **Jyotisha (Astronomy and Astrology):** Jyotisha involves timekeeping and astronomical calculations. It determines the proper timing (muhurat) for rituals by observing celestial movements.

Vedangas provided the linguistic and scientific framework required to decode Vedic knowledge systematically and accurately.

Upavedas

The Upavedas are secondary scriptures associated with the practical application of Vedic knowledge. Each Upaveda is linked to a specific Veda and deals with empirical sciences:

Ayurveda (Medicine): Associated with Rigveda; focused on health, wellness, and medical treatment.

Dhanurveda (Military Science): Associated with Yajurveda; included martial arts, weaponry, and war tactics.

Gandharvaveda (Music and Fine Arts): Associated with Samaveda; covered vocal and instrumental music, dance, and aesthetics.

Sthapatyaveda (Architecture and Engineering): Associated with Atharvaveda; dealt with civil engineering, town planning, and sculpture.

These texts reflected the broadening of Vedic education into applied sciences and technology, showing an early blend of theoretical and practical knowledge.

Shad-darshanas

Darshanas are systems of Indian philosophy which sought different means to perceive the truth. The word 'Darshana' means "to see" or "vision", indicating a way of understanding reality. Some systems accepted the scriptural authority of Vedas. These systems are called as ***Astika Systems***, whereas those systems which do not accept the scriptural authority of Vedas are called as ***Nastika Systems***.

Among the Nastikas were Gautama Buddha and Vardhamana Mahavira, who founded **Buddhism** and **Jainism** respectively. The other two Nastika schools were **Ajivika**, whose followers believed that everything was already predetermined by fate and **Charvaka**, whose followers believed in materialistic world. Charvaka's believe that there is nothing other than the body and we are just the body. When the body dies, there is no after life.

There are six main *Astika* systems known together as *Shad-darshanas.* These are:

Nyaya – This system deals with rules of logic and epistemology.

Vaisheshika – This system believes that the world is made up of infinite atoms which combine to form earth, fire, air and water.

Samkhya – This system believes that the world is made of the dual nature – *Purusha (spirit)* and *Prakriti (matter)*.

Yoga – This system deals with practices related to the regulation of mind which further enhance the inward perception of the individual.

Mimamsa – This system deals with the philosophical explanation of the Vedic rituals.

Vedanta (UttaraMimamsa) – Vedanta explores the **philosophy of the Upanishads**, particularly the nature of Brahman (absolute reality) and Atman (soul). It supports ideas like **non-dualism (Advaita)**, emphasizing that the individual soul and universal soul are one. There is a non-separateness between God and us – we are not – 'a' (not) + 'dvaita' (two) - *Advaita* (अद्वैत). The purpose of life is to again establish or realize this oneness with God. Once this oneness is established, we attain what is called *moksha*, *mukti*, or freedom. Based on the principles of Vedanta, the philosophical school founded by Adi Shankracharya in 8th century is known as Advaita Vedanta. Over a period of time, this philosophy came to be challenged by other scholars. In the 11th century, Ramanujan Acharya founded a Vishist Advaita and in the 13th century, Madhvacharya founded Dvaita Vedanta and in the 16th century Vallabh Acharya founded the school of Sudh Advaita.

These philosophical systems were integral to ancient Indian higher education and promoted **critical inquiry, disciplined reasoning, and spiritual reflection**. Each system developed distinct methodologies and perspectives but shared a commitment to self-knowledge, liberation (moksha), and logical inquiry.

Dharma Shastras

The **Dharma Shastras** are ancient Sanskrit texts that laid down the principles of **ethical conduct, legal procedures, and social duties** in Hindu society. They are part of **Smriti literature** and aimed to define dharma—the moral and legal order of individual and collective life.These texts guided individuals based on their **varna (social class)** and **ashrama**

(stage of life), covering areas like **family law, inheritance, property rights, criminal law, and penance**. They also outlined ideal behavior, rituals, and societal responsibilities, forming the basis of ancient Indian jurisprudence.

Prominent Dharma Shastras

1. **Manusmriti (Laws of Manu):** Considered the most authoritative Dharma Shastra, Manusmriti codified rules related to varna (caste duties), ashrama (stages of life), family and inheritance law, ritual purity, and punishment for crimes. It emphasized a hierarchical and patriarchal social structure, granting primacy to the Brahmin class and male authority.

2. **Yajnavalkya Smriti:** More progressive and systematic than Manusmriti, this text focused on judicial procedures, inheritance laws, and property rights. It also emphasized the role of the king as the upholder of dharma and introduced concepts like legal documentation and the importance of evidence in disputes.

3. **Narada Smriti:** Specializing in civil and procedural law, NaradaSmriti outlined rules for court procedures, contracts, debt, partnership, and theft. It is one of the few Dharma Shastras that focused almost exclusively on secular matters and had practical implications for judicial administration.

Puranas

The term 'Purana' literally means ancient or old. The Puranas are a sacred part of Hindu literature and they contain folk tales, legends and myths. They are divided into two parts – the Mahapuranas and Upa Puranas. Written in Sanskrit, there are 18 narratives in each category. The texts of Puranas are also translated into Tamil and other Indian languages.

You must have heard about 'The Ramayana' and 'The Mahabharata', these texts come under the 'Itihasa' or 'history'. Even though majority of the Hindus accept that every single event mentioned in the epics may not have happened exactly as described, they do believe that the events, people, kingdoms, and dynasties were all real.

The Puranas belong to the same class as the Itihasa. The word 'Purana' is a Sanskrit word and it means ancient or old. The Puranas were also compiled by Vyasa. These were written to popularise the Vedas. Basically, they contain the essence of the Vedas. Primarily, written in Sanskrit, Puranas are like an encyclopaedia of stories, with legends of gods, heroes, folk tales, pilgrims, astronomy, theories and philosophies.

The aim of the Puranas is to generate devotion to God among people by giving them concrete examples, stories, legends, kings and great men, allegories and chronicles of great historical events. Thus, the Puranas were created for the ordinary people who could not understand complex philosophy and who could not study the Vedas. Because of their simplicity, the Puranas are popular even today. The major Puranas are known as the ***Mahapuranas***. The most popular Puranas are the Srimad Bhagavata and the Vishnu Purana. The 18 Mahapuranas include the Vishnu, Narada, Bhagavata, Garuda, Padma, Varaha, Matsya, Kurma, Linga, Shiva, Skanda, Agni, Brahmanda, Brahmavaivarta, Markandeya, Bhavishya, Vamana and Brahma.

The lesser known Puranas are called as ***Upa-Puranas***. These are Sanat Kumar, Narasimha, Briha-Naradiya, Shiv-Rahasya, Durvasa, Kapila, Vamana, Bhargava, Varuna, Kalika, Samba, Nandi, Surya, Parasara, Vasishtha, Ganesha, Mudgala and Hamsa Puranas.

Essentially, the Puranas serve to make these ancient teachings relevant and accessible to many people in India.Through stories, legends, chronicles of historical events, and concrete examples of devotion to God, the Puranas guide individuals on how to lead a dharmic, happy, and fulfilled life.

By now, we know that in Hinduism, knowledge is important and reading scriptures helps us become more aware especially as students. It enables us to understand the objects or surroundings around us. Knowledge can also be defined as something which is correct and true across time. As students, we can gain knowledge and teachings of God through the Vedas, particularly the Upanishads. You must have heard from your elders about Goddess Saraswati, who is considered the goddess of knowledge, music, art, speech, wisdom and learning. The earliest mention of Saraswati as a goddess is in the oldest Veda, the Rigveda. She was a significant goddess in the Vedic period and still holds a special place in the hearts of all students. Thus, Vedas transform a person into a more knowledgeable and balanced being.

The Vedas are not only religious texts but they also embody the cultural heritage of India. Studying the Vedas enables students to connect with their roots and understand the ancient wisdom that has shaped their culture. It fosters a sense of pride and identity while promoting cultural preservation.

02

Vedas – The Backbone of Everything You Know

Vedas are hymns devoted to the forces of nature. The term Vedas comes from the Sanskrit word 'Vid', which means vidya or knowledge. The Vedas help humans to become aware of their true selves. The knowledge provided by the Vedas was received directly from the universal power. It is the Vedas that help us understand or distinguish the difference between what is right and what is wrong. The main aim of these texts is to help the seeker find balance in different aspects of his/her life to reach higher spiritual goals.

Did you notice that we call the Vedas 'texts' and not simply 'books'? You must have understood why it is like that. The reason is that they weren't really 'books' - no one wrote them out or printed them on paper/birch bark/palm leaves and then bound the pages together. Vedic knowledge was initially transmitted orally from guru to shishya and preserved through rigorous memorization, a method that ensured its continuity across generations.

Essence of the Vedas

For your initial reference, here is a quick snapshot of what the Vedas are all about:

1. You are not your body or your mind. You are something deeper than your deepest feelings, wiser than your wisest thoughts, you are that which is unchangeable, invincible, perfectly blissful and eternal.
2. The universe – or the universe as it appears to you – is a real or unreal as you want it to be, given that YOU are constructing it, constantly, in your mind; it exists because YOU are conscious of it, it has no independent existence apart from you.
3. The purpose of human life, according to Vedas, is *darshana*, which means seeing. Seeing what exactly? The truth about ourselves – and everyone.

And what is this truth?

That, despite what we see when we look in the mirror, we are not the things we can see, hear and feel, like our bodies or our breadth.

4. Every living being has a soul, known as *jivatman*.
5. Vedanta is the knowledge or awareness (*jnana*) about the relationship between the *jivatman* and the *paramatman*.
6. There is the cycle of worldly existence, *samsara* and the goal is to become free from this cycle by attaining emancipation (*moksha*).
7. Until one has attained emancipation, one is bound by *karma*.

In addition to enquiring into these insights in deep detail, the Vedas address the following quintessential questions about life, *jiva* and the world:

- Who am I?
- Where did the universe come from?
- What is the purpose of my life?
- Is there a God? And if yes, who/where is God?
- How to be happy all the time?
- What is death?

When Vyasa compiled the Vedas, he categorised Vedas into 4 types. In chronological order, they are the Rig Veda, the Yajur Veda, the Sama Veda and the Atharva Veda. It is believed that Vedas were a part of curriculum during ancient times in universities such as Nalanda. These sacred texts were taught as 'Gyan' by the Gurus to their shishyas. Let us understand each of these a little better.

(A) Rig Veda

Rig Veda is the oldest of all the Vedic scriptures. Though the date of the composition of Vedas cannot be confirmed as the texts were passed down orally through generations in the Vedic period, it is believed that the written form dates back to around 1600 BCE. This was done using a precise and elaborate technique. The Sanskrit word 'Rig' means to praise and 'Veda' refers to knowledge. The Rig Veda is divided into 10 books or mandalas. It has 1,028 hymns and 10,600 verses. These hymns are considered to be the reflections of the divine vibrations that the sages experienced. They are chanted to invoke the God to provide strength and courage at all times.

Also, the Rig Veda has the famous Gayatri Mantra and the Mahamrityunjaya mantra. While the Gayatri mantra is a salutation to 'Sun', the Mahamrityunjaya mantra is a prayer to Lord Shiva. We have already known the Gayatri mantra, now let's go deep into the Mahamrityunjaya mantra. Also known as the Rudra mantra, this mantra refers to the furious aspect of Lord Shiva. **The word Mahamrityunjaya is made up of three Hindi words: "Maha," which means great, "Mrityun," which means death; and "Jaya," which means victory, here, implying victory over death. It is believed that this mantra was found by Rishi Markandeya, one of the greatest saints of India**. The mantra is considered beneficial for mental, emotional and physical health of a person. It is a moksha mantra which bestows longevity and a disease-free life. The mantra is addressed to Lord Shiva for warding off untimely death. This great mantra is chanted for conquering death as it protects against all threats. Not only this, but it also eases the process of release at the time of death. This mantra is chanted to relieve one from troubles and miseries. The chanting of this mantra results in freedom from hardships. It is anticipated that regular reciting of this mantra allows to attain eternal happiness and prosperity. The powerful mantra goes like this:

महामृत्युंजय मन्त्र:

ॐ त्र्यम्बकं यजामहे	**Om tryambakam yajamahe**
सुगन्धिं पुष्टिवर्धनम्	**sugandhim pusti vardhanam**
उर्वारुकमिव बन्धनान्	**Urvarukamiva bandhanan**
मृत्योर्मुक्षीय मामृतात् ॥	**mrtyor mukshiya mamritat॥**

The essence of this mantra is - We worship Lord Shiva, the Trinitarian, who nurtures this world with his power, we pray to him to liberate us from this bond of birth and death and grant us salvation. Just as a cucumber, after being ripened from its vine, automatically falls free and falls on the ground, similarly we too should aim to free ourselves from all the bonds of birth and death from this vine-worldly life.

Besides the Rig Veda, this mantra is also found in the Yajur Veda and the Atharva Veda. According to some Puranas, the Mahamrityunjaya Mantra has been used by many *rishis*, whereas the Gayatri Mantra is meant for purification and spiritual guidance, the Mahamrityunjaya Mantra is meant for healing, rejuvenation and nurturance.

The Rig Veda encourages the chanting of mantra. It also talks about worshipping the five forces of nature - Earth (Prithvi), water (Jal), fire (Agni), wind (Vayu), and sky (Akash). Apparently, it is believed that the human body is also made up of these five elements.

Deities of Rigveda

The main deity who was worshipped in the Rigveda was Indra. He was the chief god during the Rig Vedic age. He was also known as the king of gods & lord of heaven. He is the god of thunder and rain and a great warrior. Agni, the second most important god of Rigveda, is the god of fire & sacrifice.

The third most important god of Rigveda is Soma. He is the god of the Soma plant, which was used in religious ceremonies.

Rudra is the fourth most important god of Rigveda. He is the god of wind & storm. Vishnu is the fifth most important god of Rigveda. He is the preserver of the universe. Varuna is the sixth most important god of Rigveda. He is the god of water & rain. Mitra, the seventh most important god of Rigveda, is the god of friendship & alliance.

The Rig Veda also contains an explanation of the origin of the universe, the purpose of human existence and the way life functions. It attempts to answer deep existential questions that are rarely addressed. Thus, the Rig Veda provides answers to questions that bother most of us. If we talk about science and its theories, our learned scientists provide us with the Big Bang theory. This theory states that the universe began as just a single point, then expanded and stretched to grow as large as it is right now, and it is still stretching. You must be knowing that according to Stephen W. Hawking, there was no time before the Big Bang and time began at the moment of the Big Bang. Surprisingly, the Rig Veda, also shares a somewhat similar theory. It is discussed in the Nasadiya Sukta, also called as the hymn of creation, the 129th hymn (sukta) in the tenth book (mandal) of Rigveda. It is concerned with cosmology and the origin of the universe. The Nasadiya Sukta starts and ends with questions regarding creation. It does not say that God made the universe, the stars, the sun, the moon, the earth, the plants, the animals and the humans, but on the contrary, asks how anyone could know how and when creation happened, because everything and all beings including the Devas or Gods, would have appeared only after the universe came into existence.

Interesting or may be confusing! One needs to go deep into the Vedas to understand these concepts.

In addition to this, the Rig Veda also teaches that the purpose of our existence is to experience true happiness. Many of us spend our entire lives pursuing happiness but are not at peace. To make sure that we are on the right track towards achieving contentment in life, we need to differentiate between our necessities and desires and create a balance in our lives. Subsequently, we need to start working towards fulfilment of our needs as soon as possible. According to Rig Veda, wealth has to be won by deeds of glory.

(B) Sama Veda

Sama means 'melody' and Veda means 'knowledge'. Thus, Sama Veda is also known as the Veda of 'Melodies' or 'Chants'. It is similar to Rig Veda, which means that it has the same meaning and content of the Rig Veda but it is made to sing and not read. It is the shortest Veda and has 1875 verses out of which 1771 verses are from Rig Veda. The remaining 99 are its original verses. It was created to sing the ceremonies offered to Gods. It is believed that the Sama Veda was compiled during 1200 or 1000 BCE. It holds a divine status in the Hindu tradition. Thus, Sama Veda helps a person attain spiritual evolution through music.

The Sama Veda also has commentaries on the syllable Om or Aum, which is a sacred utterance in Hinduism. According to Sama Veda, Om has been described as the source of being and is considered superior to any ritual.

The Sama Veda offers us some wonderful teachings. If followed, these provide the essence of life. These may genuinely help you as a student to understand the nitty-gritty of life.

- Cleanliness can help you stay away from diseases.
- Virtuous deeds can help you become great.
- Do not have double standards as it never lets you experience happiness.
- Your knowledge can let you attain supremacy.
- Night is to rest and relax.
- Self-control makes you the master.
- Never be in the company of those who hate knowledge.
- Do participate in auspicious activities.
- Every day is a battle, you have to fight bravely.
- Follow the path of truthfulness.

(C) Yajur Veda

Yajur means 'worship' or 'sacrifice' and Veda means 'knowledge'. You may be surprised to know that though this is the third Veda, it was the most used Vedic scripture by the ancient priests. The reason behind this is that this Veda is like a step-by-step guide that provides the correct way of performing religious ceremonies and rituals. It has all ritual-offering mantras and chants. The priests chant these mantras alongside the person who performs the ritual. Thus, Yajur Veda contains rules and mantras to be uttered during a Yagna or Havana.

The Yajur Veda has two main sections - the **Shukla Yajur Veda** (White Yajur Veda) and the **Krishna Yajur Veda** (Black Yajur Veda). The Shukla Yajur Veda mostly has verses that are recited during rituals, whereas the Krishna Yajur Veda has prose passages that discuss how the rituals are performed.

We have just mentioned Yagna as a popular ritual in the Vedic times but what exactly is a Yagna? "Yagna" is a form of worship, in which offerings are made to different deities in a prescribed and systematic manner in order to seek their blessings. It is done in the presence of sacred fire or agni.

The reason behind organising Yagna is to please the deities so that they assist the worshippers in achieving their goals and desires in life. Yagnas are usually done with the help of qualified priests. So, Yajurveda is basically the veda of 'yajush'. Yajush means worship and sacrifice. It contains sacrificial formulas in prose.

Vedic Yagna is helpful as it connects an individual with the Almighty. The sound releasing from the chants and the mantras is mentally and spiritually relaxing. Yagna purifies the mind, body, soul, and atmosphere. It clears out all the negativity from one's life. The atmosphere around the site of yagna becomes fresh and healthy as smoke from medicinal herbs kills all the disease causing germs. It helps to give a peaceful and happy life, which has less of anger and hatred. It infuses one with love, calmness and generosity. It reduces sufferings and cleanses away all our sins.

Now, in the Vedic ages, there were several types of yagnas. To start with, there were daily fire yagnas performed at home or outside, there were fortnightly yagnas to celebrate the new moon, four-monthly yagnas to celebrate the start of a new season, yagnas to rejoice a good harvest or a yagna to pray for rain. There were also special yagnas to mark birth, marriage or death. Besides these, there were mega yagnas that were performed by kings to celebrate their victory or mark similar special occasions. Let's read about that three most important Yagnas of the Vedic times:

- **The Ashwamedha** – The best known of the three, the Ashwamedha Yagna, featured 'ashwa' or a horse as 'medha' or offering to the gods. Thus, it was a Vedic horse sacrifice ritual, which was performed by rulers to prove their imperial sovereignty. It was meant to establish a king as the undisputed ruler of his empire. In this ritual, a horse was left to wander for a year. Anyone could challenge the authority of the king by fighting with the warriors who travelled with the horse. If no one stopped the horse in that particular year, the horse would be sacrificed and the king would be declared as the undisputed ruler of the entire territory. Only a powerful king performed the Ashwamedha yagna, not only because it was expensive but also because it involved taking on several hostile armies during the period.

One of the sacred scriptures of Hindus, the Ramayana also has a story related to the Ashwamedha yagna. It is said that years after Rama had sent Sita away to the forest, he performed the Ashwamedha Yagna. Since the yagna required Sita to be present there, and since Rama had never stopped thinking of her as his beloved, he got a statue of Sita cast in gold at the site.

The consecrated horse was set free to roam where it willed, and no one dared to stop it. Now, two young challengers at the forest hermitage of sage Valmiki captured the horse and also took on Rama's soldiers with great skill and valour. They defeated the army sent by Rama so badly that Rama himself was forced to intervene. The two youngsters were none other than Lava and Kusha, Rama and Sita's sons.

- **The Rajasuya -** Once again, this yagna was an elaborate yagna that was performed to establish that a king was indeed the single and unchallenged big boss of his kingdom. It was usually performed by Kshatriya kings desirous of liberation. Only once in many centuries did a king acquire enough power and prominence to claim that he could perform a Rajasuya Yagna. It was a ritual to transform a king into an emperor. It was like sending out the message that a certain king has become fit and powerful enough to be the king of kings, so either others accept him or fight with him. The time required for the performance of this yagna was roughly three years.

To start the yagna, invitations were sent out to a whole lot of kings, princes and chieftains, both inside and outside the kingdom. If a king accepted the invitation and attended the yagna, it meant that he had accepted the host King as his ruler and would be loyal to him in future. There is a mention of the Rajasuya Yagna in the Mahabharta where king Yudhisthira performs the yagna on Narad's insistence.

Recently, Rajasuya Yagna was performed in 2018 by Brahmana Seva Sangam, wishing the Chief Minister of Telangana, K Chandrashekhar to become the next Prime Minister of India.

- **The Soma**– This yagna was different from the two yagnas that we mentioned just now as this was meant to be a yagna performed for the welfare of humanity. There was no horse involved in this yagna, but there was, huge quantity of soma, which is the king of all medicinal herbs. Soma drinks were offered as oblations to gods. It was believed to strengthen and rejuvenate the gods and put them in a good mood. The yagna itself was meant to clean the air of toxins and pollutants. The yagna was a guarantee for health, happiness and prosperity. This yagna was highly spiritual and effective and needed six days to complete.

In today's day and age, while the Ashwamedha yagnas have not been performed from ages, it is the Soma Yagna that continues to have a special place in the hearts of many Hindus. The Soma Yagna is performed from time to time especially before auspicious occasions. Among Hindus, before any auspicious occasion, it is believed that one should remember God and only then the work will be successful.

Have you noticed that whenever any havan is performed at your home or any other place, we always repeat the word 'swaha' at the end of the mantra? Have you ever thought what does this word mean? Swaha is a Sanskrit word, which has more than one translation. In Tibetan language, it means 'so be it' or 'well said'. In Hinduism, swaha means delivery in the right way. Hindus believe that no yagna is successful until the havan is accepted by the deities. In the Rig Veda, swaha appears as a feminine noun which probably means an offering to Agni, the fire god. Thus, swaha basically teaches how one should make offerings to God. The word demands complete surrender, humility and sweetness full of emotions, after establishing oneself in wisdom, without ego and attachment.

So, after having a glance of the important yagnas, let's move back to Yajur Veda, which in comparison to Rig Veda is much simpler in language. There are 40 Adhyayas and 1875 Verses in the Yajur Veda. Several verses of the Yajur Veda reflect the religious and social life of the Vedic people. One of the most popular hymns from the Yajur Veda is the **Shanti Mantra** (ॐ द्यौः शान्तिरन्तरिक्षं शान्तिः पृथिवी शान्तिरापः शान्तिरोषधयः शान्तिः । वनस्पतयः शान्तिर्विश्वेदेवाः शान्तिर्ब्रह्म शान्तिः सर्वं शान्तिः शान्तिरेव शान्तिः सा मा शान्तिरेधि ॐ शान्तिः शान्तिः शान्तिः ॥), often recited at the beginning and end of Hindu rituals, and the Gayatri Mantra, which is a popular mantra for meditation. It is considered to bless the reciter with spiritual and intellectual powers.

(D) Atharva Veda

The Atharva Veda is the last of the four Vedas. It is different from the other three Vedas as while they deal with matters of other world, the gods and nature, the Atharva Veda is more worldly. It is related to both worldly happiness and spiritual knowledge.. It deals with topics like leading a long and healthy life, avoiding sorrow, warding off illness etc. Unlike the other three Vedas, the Atharva Veda is not concerned with sacred rituals but it helps to solve daily problems. Thus, the Atharva Veda is most diverse in nature as compared to the other three Vedas. It deals with religion and cultural aspect of society and provides knowledge about the same.

The Atharva Veda has 20 books that contain hymns, chants, spells and prayers. It teaches the importance of spiritual knowledge and makes a person understand the true nature of self. It provides a person with a deep understanding of the self, and this, in turn, helps a person or a student to overcome negative emotions and achieve inner peace.

Another important contribution of the Atharva Veda is the discussion about various diseases, their causes and treatments. Various medicinal plants, mantra therapy, water therapy, sun rays treatment, psychological treatment and other relevant discussions are in prominence in the Atharva Veda. In fact, in the Indian medical system, Ayurveda is a sub-branch of the Atharva Veda. It discusses various methods of enjoying good health and long life, and is also the most popular Veda.

In addition to this, the Atharva Veda also talks about helping others and contributing to the society, both of which give a sense of purpose and fulfilment in life. It recognizes the importance of nature and environment. People can learn to appreciate the beauty of nature and understand the interconnectedness of all living beings. The Atharva Veda encourages the pursuit of wisdom and knowledge. It motivates students to develop a lifelong love for learning and strives to gain knowledge and understanding of the world around them.

- **Rig-Veda** "Knowledge of the Hymns of Praise", for recitation.
- **Sama-Veda** "Knowledge of the Melodies", for chanting.
- **Yajur-Veda** "Knowledge of the Sacrificial formulas", for liturgy.
- **Atharva-Veda** "Knowledge of the Magic formulas", named after a kind of group of priests.

The Four Vedas

The Vedas contain complex philosophical ideas and debates. Engaging with Vedic texts encourages students to think critically, analyze concepts, and engage in intellectual discourse. This develops their analytical and reasoning skills, fostering intellectual growth.

03

Upanishads- Outlining the Universal Knowledge

Now, let's learn something about the Upanishads. We are aware that these are the concluding parts of the Vedas and that is why they are also called as Vedanta. They are the most sacred and provide the easiest way to understand the philosophies and complexities of life.

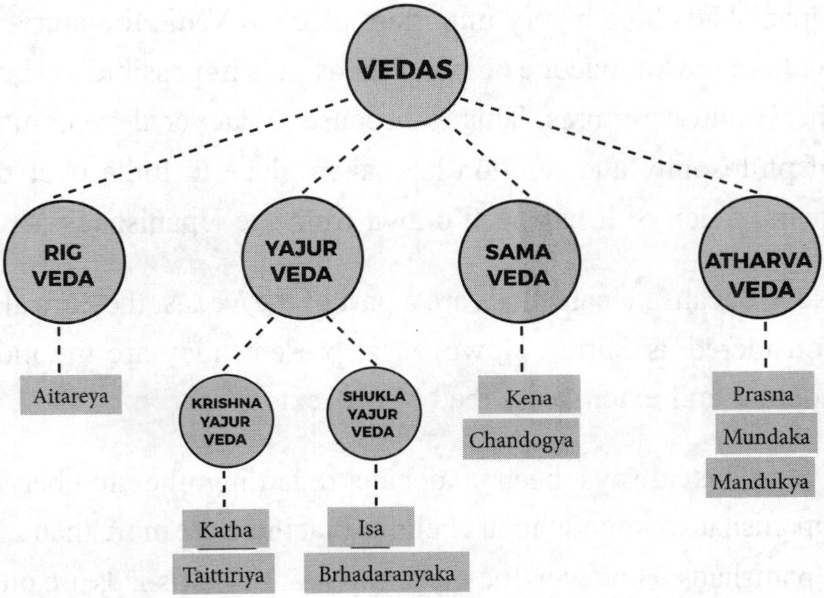

The 4 Vedas and the 10 main Upanishads

Just like the names of other scriptures, the word Upanishad has come from Sanskrit. It is a combination of three Sanskrit syllables – *upa*, which means, 'to move closer to'; *ni*, which means 'at a lower level'; and *shad*, which means 'to sit'. So, the literal meaning of the word "Upanishad" is 'to sit close to someone, at a lower level.' That is why the Upanishads have always been seen as stories, which had deep-rooted lessons, shared between a teacher and a student. They are considered as secret teachings imparted at such sittings. It is also interesting to know that because of these teachings were secret and mysterious, it was not easy for a student to obtain this wisdom from the teacher. He had to really prove his worthiness to the teacher to gain this knowledge.

Upanishads hold a very important place in Vedic literature, as without the knowledge of Upanishads, it is impossible to know the Hindu scriptures. This is because whatever development of philosophy and religion has taken place in India over the years, much of it has been drawn from the Upanishads.

Now, because Upanishads are a part of the Vedas, they are also considered as Shruti. However, at present, they are the most popular and extensively read Vedic texts.

There has always been a debate regarding the number of Upanishads. Some scholars believe that there are more than 200 Upanishads. However, the most important Upanishads are only 108, out of which 10 are considered the Principal Upanishads. These are believed to form the core of Hindu philosophical and spiritual thought. Out of these 108 Upanishads, 10 are from the Rigveda, 51 from the Yajurveda, 16 Upanishads from the Samaveda and finally 31 from the Atharvaveda. In Muktika Upanishad, Lord Ram gave a list of 108 Upanishads to Hanuman through a hymn.

The Upanishads share the central theme of Vedas and speak of the highest goal or Supreme bliss. The lines given below found in the Upanishads are often recited as a general prayer:

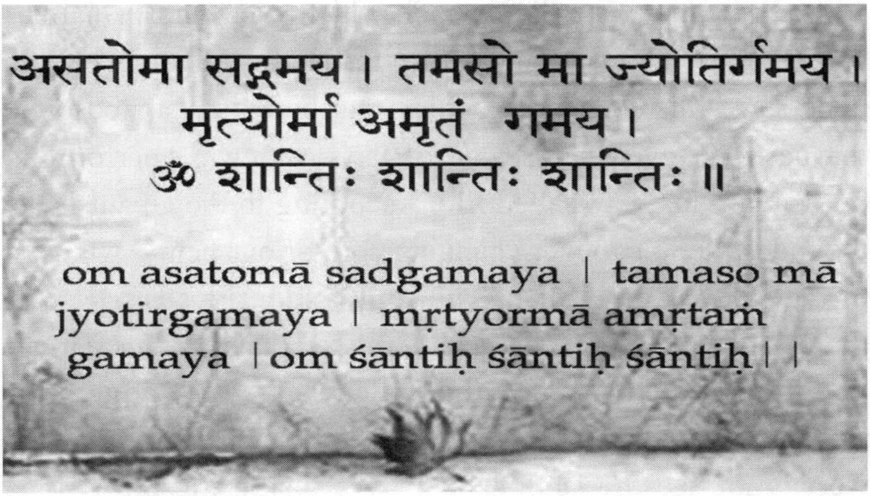

This is a Shanti mantra to the supreme god in which we pray to him to lead us from the unreal to the real, from darkness to light and from death to immortality. We ask for peace, peace, peace!

Philosophy of the Vedas

The best part about Upanishads is that they provide answers to questions which always bother the human mind - Who Am I? What is this Universe? Why are we born? etc. It is fascinating to know that the Upanishads, though thousands of years old, still hold huge relevance in our lives. The Vedas explore the nature of reality, the self, and the universe, offering profound spiritual insights. They provide guidance on meditation, self-realization, and the path to enlightenment. Students who delve into the Vedas can cultivate a deeper understanding of themselves and the world around them, fostering spiritual growth. Let's look at some important philosophies or lessons provided by the Upanishads:

1. Atman: There is a divine soul, which every individual has and which is eternal. This soul is called as Atman. You can understand this concept like this - Our body is just a costume that has been given to us so that we can wear it while performing our role in this play called life. According to the Upanishads, the indestructible, never-changing core of our being, which is the actual 'I' is the Atman. **The soul is like the electricity in an electrical gadget. Electricity passes through this gadget and infuses life into it. Without electricity, the gadget is of no use. This electricity is invisible to us. In a similar way, we cannot see the soul, which lives inside the body. It is like butter which remains completely dissolved in milk**. Most Hindu philosophical schools consider that the body is made of matter and the Atman is made of non-matter. All things around us are physical or material, they are all made of atoms. Atman is beyond all these. In some sense, atman is life inside the matter.

2. Samsara or the Cycle of Rebirth: The word Samsara in Sanskrit means "wandering." It is the cycle of being. According to Samsara, when you die, it's only your body that dies. Your soul doesn't, it simply moves on and enters another body. If your deeds are good in life, you are born again, as a human and can proceed further on your journey to ultimate happiness. If you haven't been good, you might turn into some other creature, maybe a bird or a cockroach. This means you may have to work your way up the hierarchy of creatures, until you are human again, and have the ability to distinguish between right and wrong. Thus, the wheel of life continues to turn, and nothing is ever stationary.

According to the 'Svetasvatara Upanishad', this vast universe is a wheel, the wheel of Brahman. Upon it are all creatures that are subject to birth, death and rebirth. Round and round, it turns and never stops.

3. Karma or Action: Next comes the Karma, a word, which you must have heard several times. It literally means, 'action, work, or deed.' It is believed that every action has a consequence, so one must act very carefully. You may escape punishment for a bad action for some time but eventually you will have to pay for it. Karma or the karmic cycle says that whatever you do today will have an influence on your life tomorrow and circling back to the concept of Samsara, what you do today will also influence your next life. This reminds me of a Doha from Tulsidas' *Ramcharitmanas,* which says,

काहु न कोउ सुख दुख कर दाता।

निज कृत करम भोग सबु भाता।।

No one gives anyone joy or sorrow. Everyone gets the result of their karma alone.

4. Dharma: According to the Upanishads, the concept of dharma refers to truth, order and fulfilling one's duty. It says that each of us has been assigned a role to play in this life. Now, this may be of a scholar, thinker, leader, follower, anyone. That role takes on different shades as life moves on. You start as a student, then become a professional. When you are born, you are a child, in a few years you become parent to a child. To put it in simple words, our role keeps changing with time but it is our duty and responsibility to play our role to the best of our potential in every phase of life. Also, we should not complain and compare ourselves with others, something which we often do – Why am I not as good looking as he is? Such thoughts should have no place in our life.

Thus, Dharma encourages us to fulfil our role in the society we live and that too, to the best of our abilities. We should equip ourselves with respect, empathy, grace and courage.

5. Moksha: In Sanskrit, Moksha means 'liberation' or enlightenment. It refers to the ultimate end of suffering. It is a very powerful concept mentioned in the Upanishads. We all know that human life is full of pain and trouble. The final goal of human life is to look for lasting happiness, which happens only when a person breaks free of samsara's golden chains. If you believe in performing your Dharma and doing good deeds in this lifetime, you may have a chance of getting liberated, maybe after two million more lifetimes' of good behaviour.

6. Maya: Being hooked to Netflix is a very common thing for people today. When we consume its content with all our heart and also our organs of perception – eyes, ears, nose, mouth, and skin – we are tuned to believe that everything is so bright and beautiful, that it is tempting and demanding. We become confident that what is shown is the real thing, however, it is just an illusion. So, we need not let people play with our minds. We need to understand that this world is an illusion or maya and it is not the ultimate reality.

7. Brahman: The ultimate reality or ultimate truth that underlies everything in this universe is called the Brahman.

There is only one Universal Energy or one Supreme consciousness, that is inside each one of us. It is also all around us. We may call it as Shakti, Shoonya, Allah, Yahweh, Ahura Mazda, God, our own individual choices but according to the Upanishads, this supreme, all-pervading energy is called the Brahman (say Bruhm-mum.)

8. Knowledge: The Upanishads emphasize on the importance of knowledge and understanding in the pursuit of spiritual enlightenment. They motivate the seeker to question and explore their own beliefs and assumptions. The hymns, poetry, and philosophical ideas in the Vedas can inspire students and stimulate their creativity. The profound verses and vivid descriptions found in the Vedas can ignite the students' imagination and encourage students to think outside the box, fostering artistic and literary pursuits.

9. Yoga: The practice of yoga, which involves physical postures, meditation and breathing exercises, has come to us from the Upanishads. Yoga can help an individual attain spiritual growth and liberation. It is a way to achieve spiritual self-realization and liberation. The practice of yoga can help any individual achieve a state of inner peace and enlightenment.

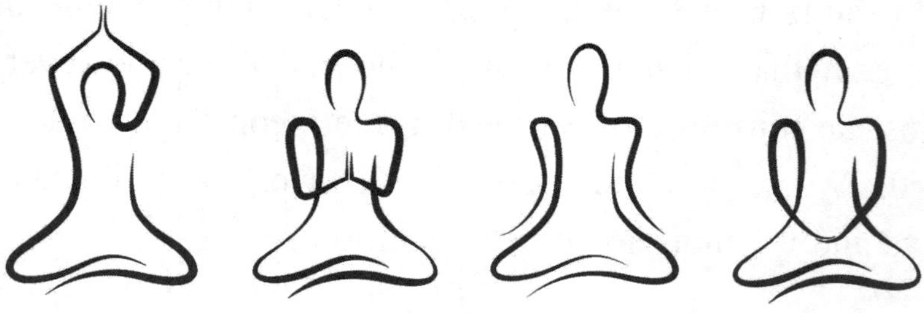

10. You are God: According to the Upanishads, you were not created by God, but you are God. You need to understand that Atman is Brahman, or, you are God. Finding it a little difficult to digest? But that is what our scriptures say. It's not only for you but also for everybody around you. That means, everyone around you is also God. They may be of different skin colours, may have weird ways of speaking, eating or worshipping, but everyone is God.

The Four Maha Vakyas

The Upanishads also have some great sayings, which are called as 'MahaVakyas'. These reveal the nature of Atman and Brahman. Here, maha means 'great' and vakya means 'sentence.' Mahavakyas are typically thought to be four in number. Here are these four Mahavakyas:

Prajnanam Brahma – Consciousness is Brahman (Aitareya Upanishad, Rig Veda)

Ayam Atma Brahma – This Self (Atman) is Brahman (Mandukya Upanishad, Atharva Veda)

Tat Tvam Asi – That Thou Art (Chandogya Upanishad, Sama Veda)

Aham Brahmasmi – I am Brahman (Brihadaranyaka Upanishad, Shukla Yajur Veda)

1. Prajnanam Brahma (प्रज्ञानं ब्रह्म) – "Consciousness is Brahman"

Source: Aitareya Upanishad (3.3)

"Prajnanam Brahma" states that ultimate reality is not a mere philosophical construct but the consciousness that illuminates all experience. This Mahavakya asserts that Brahman is pure awareness, the essence of all existence.

The Sanskrit word Prajna means "consciousness." This pure consciousness is eternal, unchanging reality, i.e. Brahman. This is the meaning of Prajnanam Brahma.

This saying engages with the question "Who am I?" "I am not the body. Likewise, I am not the mind. I am not the sense organs. If I go on negating like this, only the consciousness remains." That consciousness is Brahman. This is the meaning of this Mahavakya.

By meditating on "Prajnanam Brahma," one learns to detach oneself from the fleeting nature of physical existence and align with the eternal awareness that is Brahman. This insight transforms perception, allowing seekers to view the world as an expression of the divine rather than as a separate, materialistic entity.

2. Ayam Atma Brahma (अयम् आत्मा ब्रह्म)- "Atma is Brahman"

Source- Mandukya Upanishad (1-2)

Ayam Atma Brahman is found in the Mandukya Upanishad of Atharvaveda. "Ayam" means "this" which refers to self-luminous nature of the Self. This Self is Brahman that is the essence of all things in the universe. This statement represents the core philosophy of the Upanishads i.e. non-dualism. It embodies the inseparability of the self from the eternal, all-pervasive Brahman. It upholds the view that the Self is the reflection of the Ultimate Reality which is the Brahman. This identification of the Self with the Absolute Reality affirms the fact that the universal principle encompasses all beings in the universe and there is nothing that exists outside it.

3. Tat Tvam Asi (तत् त्वम् असि) – "Thou Art That"

Source: Chandogya Upanishad (6.8.7)

"Tat Tvam Asi" is one of the most powerful Mahavakyas, emphasizing the unity of the individual soul (Atman) with the Supreme Reality (Brahman). It is a declaration of non-duality, asserting that the individual self is inseparable from the highest universal principle.

Tat tvam asi, in Hinduism, is the famous expression of the relationship between the individual and the Absolute. The statement is frequently repeated in the sixth chapter of the Chandogya Upanishad (c. 600 bce) as the teacher Uddalaka Aruni instructs his son in the nature of brahman, the supreme reality. The identity expressed in this judgment was variously interpreted by the different darshans (schools) of the orthodox philosophy of Vedanta. The phrase was given its most literal interpretation by the 8th–9th-century thinker Shankara of the Advaita (Nondualist) school, for whom the statement was one of the great fundamental assertions of his doctrine of non-dualism.

This Mahavakya is the bedrock of Advaita Vedanta philosophy, which negates dualism between the creator and creation. The phrase is addressed to a disciple by his guru, teaching that the Self is identical with the Infinite, all-pervading consciousness. When fully understood, this statement dissolves the illusion of separateness and ego, leading to self-realization and enlightenment.

Sabrimala Temple, Kerala

4. Aham Brahmasmi (अहं ब्रह्मास्मि) – "I Am Brahman"

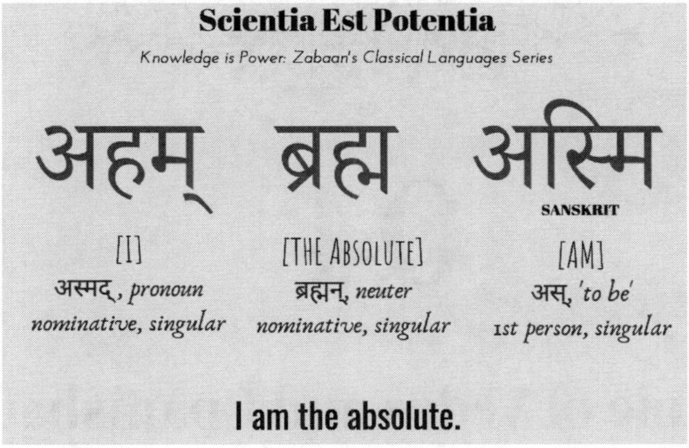

Source: Brihadaranyaka Upanishad (1.4.10)

Aham Brahmasmi is incorporated in the Brihadaranyaka Upanishad, found in Yajur Veda. Brihadaranyaka Upanishad is one of the oldest scriptures in Hinduism, and is considered to be an ancient source of spiritual wisdom.

"Aham Brahmasmi" is another foundational Mahavakya that declares the identity of the individual soul with Brahman. It is a first-person affirmation of the truth that the self is not limited to the body or mind but is, in essence, the manifestation of the infinite consciousness itself.

Representing a central theme of Advaita philosophy, Aham Brahmasmi unites the macrocosmic ideas of God and universal consciousness with the microcosmic individual expression of the Self. This mantra highlights the notion that all beings are intimately connected to universal energy and cannot be separated from it. To recite Aham Brahmasmi is to recognize that Brahman and Atman are one, and as such, there can be no ego or sense of separation.

04

Role of Vedas and Upanishads in a Student's Life

The Vedas are considered the oldest scriptures in Hinduism and contain a vast repository of knowledge. They cover various subjects such as philosophy, spirituality, ethics, mathematics, astronomy, and more. Students can gain valuable insights and wisdom from the Vedas, helping them broaden their intellectual horizons. By now, we have discussed a lot about Vedas and Upanishads, but how do we determine their importance in the life of a present-day student? The easiest way to do this is to get to know the story of Adi Shankaracharya, a great philosopher and the greatest disciple and Vedic scholar of all times.

So let's begin! In around 788 A.D., there lived a Brahmin couple, Sri Sivaguru and Aryamba at Kalady in Kerala. The couple made ardent prayers for a child to Lord Shiva. Pleased with their prayers, Shiva appeared in their dream and asked what kind of a child they wanted - whether they wanted a short-lived, intelligent son or a dull one with a long life. They chose the first option. Then, after some time, a child was born to them and they named the baby boy Shankara.

From a very young age, Shankara was intelligent and kind. Everyone was attracted towards him because of his qualities. At the age of three, he was given 'Aksharabhyas', i.e., the lessons in writing and reading. However, he lost his father, Shivaguru, early in his life. At the age of five, he was initiated in Brahmacharyam i.e., the holy thread ceremony, after which he was sent to Gurukul for learning the scriptures. As per the practice, the brahmachari had to go from house to house and take alms and submit them to his guru. Shankara performed his duty well.

Adi Shankaracharya as a child and the Crocodile

Right from his childhood, Shankara was attracted towards sanyasa, which meant leaving all worldly pleasures and leading a spiritual life. However, just like any other mother, Shankara's mother did not approve of this idea. She wanted Shankara to stay with her and lead a normal life. But destiny had something else in store. One day when Shankara was taking bath, a crocodile caught hold of his leg and pulled him down. Shankara called out to his mother for help. She came running and to her horror she found her son in the grip of the crocodile. She cried but did not know how to help her son. Sri Shankara informed his mother that his life was nearing to an end, but if he became a sanyasi, he may start a new life. He pleaded to her, 'You have never given me permission to become a sanyasi, Mother,at least give it to me now, in my last moments, so I can die happily! His mother had no choice left. ''You have my blessing!' sobbed his petrified mother. Shankaracharya started reciting the mantras of renunciation and immediately the crocodile let Shankara go. Thus, Shankara's determination and his spiritual wisdom helped him obtain permission from his mother to become a sanyasi and soon the eight-year-old set out happily on his chosen path.

It is believed that Shankara walked some 2,000 kilometres from his home in Kaladi in search of a guru before he could meet Govinda Bhagavatpada, on the banks of the river Narmada in central India. When the guru asked him who he was, the boy answered, '**Neither fire nor air nor water nor earth nor space am I, but the indestructible Atman that is hidden inside all names and forms.**' The guru was impressed with his understanding of the ultimate reality. He accepted Shankara as his disciple.

The cave where Shankara placed his Kamandala
to stop the flooding Narmada

Under the guidance of his guru, Shankara studied 'Gaudapadiya Karika', 'Brahma Sutra', Vedas, and Upanishads. Govinda was amazed to see Shankara master almost all the ancient scripts in such a short period of time, that too at a very young age. Around this time only, an intense monsoon arrived. The Narmada was in a terrible state, its dark, roiling waters rising wildly and threatening to flood a cave where Govinda was sitting in a deep meditative state or Samadhi. Everyone was in a state of panic. It was Shankara who placed his *Kamandala* at the mouth of the cave and calmly proclaimed that it would contain the flood waters within itself. To everyone's wonder, that was exactly what happened. When Govinda later heard what had happened, he blessed Shankara, saying, 'Just as you contained the flood in your little *Kamandala*, may you distil the essence of the scriptures into your writings.'

And with this started Shankara's journey of writing commentaries on the Upanishads. At the age of sixteen, he was done with the writing. After this, with his guru's blessings, Shankara started his next phase of the journey, which was to spread the good word. For the next sixteen years, Shankara walked across the length and breadth of the country, spreading the message of the philosophy called 'Advaita', which advocated the existence of the soul and the Supreme Soul.

Advaita Vedanta is the last chapter of the Vedas. The term 'Advaita' has come from the Sanskrit word which means 'not two' and the term Vedanta means 'end of knowledge'. The term Advaita Vedanta, therefore refers to 'a knowledge of that which is not two, which leads to the end of all knowledge'.. This philosophy was simple and straightforward. Shankara believed that the Supreme Soul alone is real and unchanging while the soul is a changing entity and that it does not have absolute existence. In simple words, Advaita said that there was no difference between Atman and Brahman. The literal meaning of the word "Advaita" is nonduality. In simple terms, Advaita is the absence of the duality between the Self and the Ultimate reality. Though Advaita was there even before Shankara, he was the one who is usually credited with spreading it in the best possible manner.

Shankara was also an efficient organizer. During the course of his travels, he established four monasteries or mathas, in the four corners of the country. The four mathas founded by Shankara are:

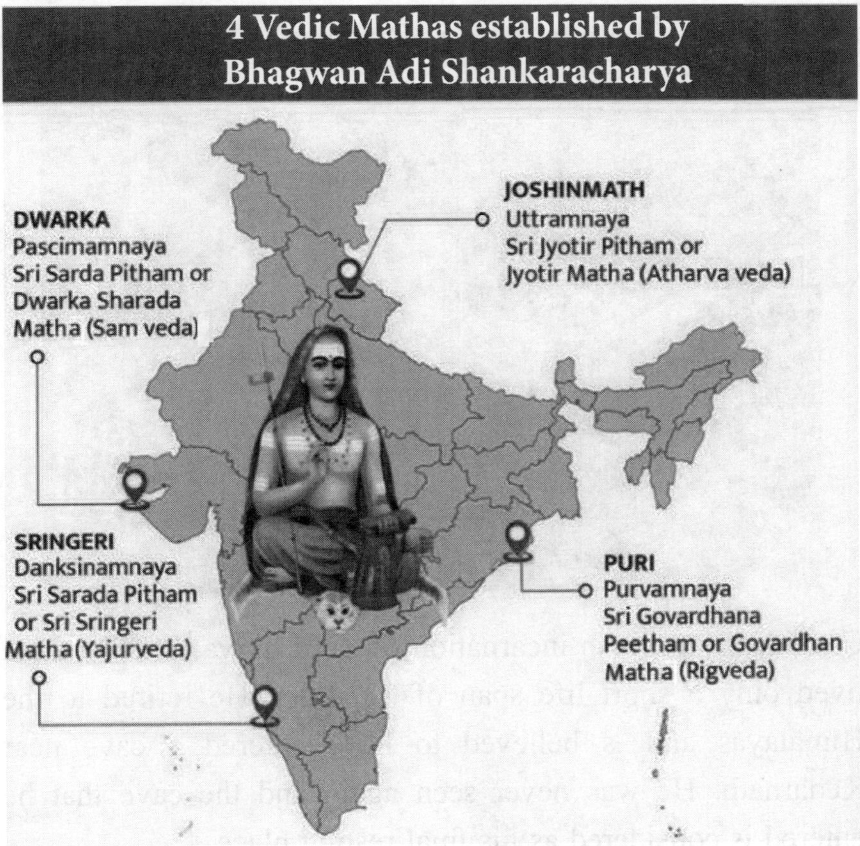

Adi Shankaracharya's Four Mathas'

- The Sringeri Matha in Sringeri - It advocates 'Aham Brahmasmi', (I am Brahman). This was formed on the basis of Yajur Veda.
- The Sarada Matha in Dwarka, Gujarat - It advocates 'Tattvamasi', (That thou art) and it was formed on the basis of Sama Veda.
- The Jyotir Matha in Badrinath - It advocates 'Ayam Atma Brahma' (This Atman is Brahman). It was formed on the basis of Atharva Veda.
- The Govardhan Matha in Puri - It advocates 'Prajnanam Brahma' (Consciousness is Brahman). It was formed on the basis of Rig Veda.

Considered to be an incarnation of Lord Shiva, Sri Shankara lived only a short life span of 32 years. He retired to the Himalayas and is believed to have entered a cave near Kedarnath. He was never seen again and the cave that he entered is considered as his final resting place.

Unfortunately, in the year 2013, this resting place or samadhi was damaged because of the Kedarnath flood. Later, at the premises of the Kedarnath Temple, his samadhi was reconstructed and in the year 2022, it was inaugurated by our Prime Minister Narendra Modi. It is amazing that even today, Shankaracharya is loved, revered and celebrated as one of the supreme teachers of the Upanishads.

Okay, so now when we have read about Adi Shankaracharya, what do we gather from his life, especially as a student? There are several lessons that a student can learn from his life. Let's quickly take a glance at some of them:

1. **Importance of Education:** Shankara was a highly educated person who mastered various branches of learning. His life teaches us the importance of education and the pursuit of knowledge.

2. **Devotion:** Shankara had complete devotion for his guru. He demonstrated this devotion by serving his guru with utmost humility and dedication. His life teaches us to do the same with our teachers and mentors in life.

3. **Dedication and Hard Work:** Shankara worked hard to gain knowledge and spread his teachings. His life teaches us the importance of dedication and hard work in achieving our goals.

4. **Open-Mindedness:** Shankara always synthesized diverse views and ideas. His approach teaches us to be open-minded and keen to adapt to different perspectives.

5. **Being Kind to Others:** Shankara was kind to others and always believed in helping others. His life teaches us the importance of service to society and the role of spirituality in social welfare.

6. **Courage:** Shankara faced many problems during his lifetime. Many Hindu priests and scholars disagreed with his views. However, he remained steadfast in his convictions and fearlessly defended his teachings. His life teaches us the importance of courage, conviction and standing up for what we believe in.

To sum up, Shankaracharya's life and teachings provide a rich legacy to all students. They encourage students to seek knowledge, work hard, remain open-minded, focus on spiritual realization and serve society.

05

What Does It Mean to be a Student?

To understand what it means to be a student, we need to know how the learned in the Vedic period divided the entire life of a person. The Vedic scriptures talk about life in four stages. These four stages are called as Ashramas. Let's look at each one of them in brief:

The Four Ashramas

- **The Brahmacharya** – The word Brahmacharya means 'celibacy'. This was the first stage where the first twenty-five years of life were to be spent as a student gaining knowledge and wisdom.
- **The Grihastha Ashram** – The literal meaning of the word grihastha is family life, so in this stage a person got married and raised a family. During this stage, it was the duty of a man to support his family, parents and other members of the community.
- **The Vanaprastha** – The word refers to a hermit, so this was the stage of retirement from worldly life starting from the age of fifty.
- **The Sanyas** – The word Sanyas means "purification of everything". This was the last stage of human life and laid importance towards leading a spiritual life.

According to Vedas, our first stage of life, Brahmacharya, is the student life. The importance of Brahmacharya is clearly explained in the Yajurveda. Today, very few of us understand this and practice it. All the Vedas and other scriptures of Hinduism lay great emphasis on Brahmacharya. In the Vedic period, a student was also known as Brahmachari. It was believed that by preserving energy, strength and vitality of mind and various organs one could lead a happy and healthy life. It was also believed that if one takes the Brahmacharya way, his mind would be cleansed off material desires and worldly passions and he would develop a sharp intellect.

The Taittriya Upanishad also highlights the value of self-study. The Upanishad includes a separate chapter which gives instructions to students during the convocation. The final lesson imparted to students before they go out in the "real world" is "Swadhaya Pravachane Cha" meaning "it is the daily duty of students to continue doing self study".

The Brahmacharya was the most important phase as it laid the foundation of life. As it was the initial years of growing, it was during this stage that a student learnt the importance of all the four goals in life. We will discuss these four goals a little later, first let us have a look at what a student's life looked like during the Vedic times.

Just like you have a school hostel these days, there was a Gurukula during that time and a student was expected to live a celibate life inside a gurukula. It was basically a traditional residential school where the students gained knowledge under the guidance of a guru. The student had to leave his home to stay with a guru to attain both spiritual and practical knowledge. The student had two duties: to learn the skills of his life and to practice unwavering devotion to his teachers. During this period, a student was called a Brahmachari as he was prepared for his future profession, as well as for his family, and social and religious life ahead.

Though admission into the gurukula was quite difficult, it was even more difficult for a student to gain the trust and confidence of the guru. A student had to serve his guru for years and convince him about his discipline, sincerity, desire, determination and level of intelligence, before he could get an opportunity to learn the advanced subjects. It was not easy to live in a gurukula. There was rigorous discipline for students. They had to live in a very harsh environment, practice celibacy and cultivate discipline and virtue. All this helped them to gain the attention and confidence of their guru. They were required to serve him personally and also undertake many menial jobs in his household to learn the virtue of humility. The gurus collected fees known as *guru dakshina* for the services their students rendered.

Thus, in ancient India, as a part of education, it was mandatory for a student to control his desires and learn to perform his obligatory duties with a sense of detachment. He had to be devoted to God. He had to overcome the obstacles of egoism, attachment and delusion. He was advised to follow the path of gods and cultivate virtue under the careful and personal tutelage of his teacher. This was to make the student walk on the path of righteousness for the rest of his life and contribute to the welfare of society. The gurus believed that if the student was grounded in dharma, he would become its upholder and would take care of its survival and continuity. To sum up, chastity, simplicity, hard work, devotion to knowledge, and spiritual reality were the ideals of a student's life.

The Four Goals of Life

Now, let's understand the four goals that we mentioned earlier. In Vedic terms, the four life goals are:

- **Dharma** – This refers to doing your duty and fulfilling your responsibilities. These may be towards your family or your community. Dharma tells a person to be morally upright in life and to live up to their potential, whether they are a student, a daughter, a father, a teacher, a boss, a doctor or a construction worker.
- **Artha**– This refers to having a goal and purpose in life, which includes the accumulation of material wealth. This may surprise you, but the Vedas were pretty practical.
- **Kama**– This goal talks about the search for pleasure. Love, affection or anything that pleased the senses or is considered enjoyable – a beautiful sunset on a beach holiday, the smell of the earth after rain, listening to a concert by your favourite pop star come under this goal.

- **Moksha**– This last goal is the quest for ultimate happiness and the most complete and blissful kind of freedom. While Dharma, Artha and Kama are all worldly pursuits, and are very important – after all, we all do live in the material world – moksha is to be detached from those very same worldly pleasures, i.e., love, hate, wealth, success and to be one with god.

Thus, it is clear that the Vedas gave great emphasis to education and learning. In the Vedic tradition, a student was expected to fulfil certain duties and responsibilities to pursue knowledge and wisdom. However, these duties are relevant even today and it is good for students to follow them. Let's quickly jot down a few pointers:

1. **Follow Dharma:** A student should follow the path of Dharma, which means he should adhere to moral and ethical values, such as honesty, integrity, respect for elders, and self-discipline.

2. **Respect Teachers:** A student should show respect and reverence towards their teachers as they are the ones who impart knowledge and wisdom. Students should obey their instructions and strive to learn as much as possible.

3. **Focus Learning:** A student should be completely devoted towards his studies. He should not get distracted. He should be disciplined, focused, and persistent in his pursuit of knowledge.

4. **Self-Control:** A student should have self-control, simplicity, and minimalism. He should have mental clarity and focus, which is essential for learning.

5. **Service to Society:** A student should engage in community service and contribute to the betterment of society. This may include activities such as volunteering or doing some charity work, or may be teaching a child from the weaker section of the society.

By following these duties, a student can develop the necessary skills, knowledge, and character to lead a successful and fulfilling life. The Vedas provide a moral and ethical framework that help students develop a strong character. They teach principles such as honesty, integrity, compassion, and respect for all beings. By imbibing these values, students can lead a balanced and virtuous life.

06

Role of a Guru in a Student's Life

We just read how during Vedic times, a student, in order to gain knowledge, had to fully devote himself to his guru. In Hinduism, a teacher or a guru is no less than God. Hinduism talks about the concept of guru or teacher as the remover of darkness. The word ‘guru’ is derived from the Sanskrit word ‘gu’ meaning darkness and ‘ru’ meaning light, which implies that the guru is the one who removes the darkness of ignorance and bestows the light of knowledge. Without serving a guru and without his blessings, it is not possible for a student to accomplish goals in life.

In the Vedic tradition, guru was a spiritual teacher who not only helped students gain knowledge but also guided them on the path of spiritual growth and realization. The guru was not only a teacher but also a mentor, a friend, a philosopher, and a guide, who helped the student overcome obstacles and challenges on the path of spiritual growth. The role of a guru in a student’s life was considered to be of utmost importance, as it was believed that without the guidance of a guru, it was impossible for a student to attain spiritual enlightenment. The guru was believed to possess a deep understanding of the mysteries of the universe and the secrets of the human soul.

The relationship between a guru and a student was considered to be sacred. It was based on trust, respect, and devotion. The student was expected to have complete devotion towards the guru and the guru took complete responsibility for the student’s spiritual progress. The guru shared knowledge through various methods - lectures, discussions, and practical demonstrations - and the student absorbed this knowledge with complete attention and dedication. The student was expected to listen attentively to the guru, ask questions, and clarify any doubts. The guru encouraged the student to develop an analytical and critical mind, so that the student should learn not only the subject matter but also understand the underlying principles.

Our Vedas not only gave us spiritual knowledge but also Ayurveda, which is the study of health and diseases, and also some performing art forms like dance and music. So, the Vedic guru also imparted these practical skills to the student. The guru taught the student how to live a virtuous and ethical life, and how to overcome the challenges and obstacles of life.

The guru-disciple relationship was not limited to the classroom but extended to all aspects of life. The guru was a mentor and guide to the student in all matters, including personal, social, and spiritual. The student was expected to develop a close relationship with the guru and seek his or her advice and guidance in all matters.

The role of the guru in a student's life was multifaceted. Here are some of the key aspects of the guru's role:

1. **Imparting Knowledge:** The primary role of the guru was to impart knowledge to the student. This knowledge was not just academic but also included spiritual and moral. The guru explained complex philosophical concepts and scriptures, and guided the student in his practical application of these concepts..
2. **Personal Guidance:** The guru provided personal guidance to the student, based on his individual needs and strengths. The guru identified the student's strengths and weaknesses and provided guidance accordingly. The guru also taught him how to overcome obstacles and challenges on the path of spiritual growth.
3. **Moral and Ethical Guidance:** The guru guided the student on moral and ethical principles, and also told them how to apply those in his daily life. The guru taught the student the importance of values such as honesty, integrity, compassion, and selflessness.
4. **Role Model:** The guru was not just a teacher but also a role model for the student. The guru would lead by example, demonstrating the virtues and qualities that the student should strive to emulate.
5. **Spiritual Awakening:** The ultimate goal of the guru was to help the student attain spiritual awakening or enlightenment.

You must be wondering that teachers may have been important during ancient ages, but today in the era of Google and

ChatGPT, they seem to hold little relevance. We can get answers online to any of our questions within a few minutes and so we do not need a teacher or a guru. But, hold on, dear students, it is not like that. Though technology can help you in your studies, it cannot be a replacement for a human teacher. A Guru will tell you what you need while Google will tell you what it knows. Whatever you learn from a Guru will be remembered for a long time while the information provided by internet has lower rate of retention. Most importantly, Google can't be your mentor or guide. A guru or a teacher plays a key role in transforming society. He may guide you in life and may contribute to building your personality or your career. Google may teach, but only a teacher can make you understand. The future of education will not be teachers versus technology, but it will be teachers combined with the best use of technology.

Part I
11 Vedic Wisdom in Stories

By now, we know that each Veda is divided into four sections, and that each Veda contains one or many Upanishads. It is the Upanishads that constitute the foundation of Vedanta so it is good to go deeper into Upanishads. It is believed that there are more than 200 Upanishads. However, the most important Upanishads are only 108. Out of these, there are 10 Principal Upanishads. They are Isha, Kena, Katha, Prashna, Mundaka, Mandukya, Taittiriya, Aitareya, Chandogya, and Brihadaranyaka. First we will understand the central message of each Upanishad and then, as we know that Upanishads were basically stories shared between gurus and shishyas, we will move on to some stories from the ten most important Upanishads.

10 Principal Upanishads

1. **ISHA UPANISHAD (YAJUR VEDA)- Karma without attachment-** This is one of the shortest Upanishad. It is in the form of a short poem consisting of 17 or 18 verses. The word Isha Vasyam translates to "enveloped by the Lord". Mahatma Gandhi once said that if all scriptures are lost and only first verse of Isha Upanishad is left, it would revive Hinduism.
2. **KENA UPANISHAD (SAMA VEDA)- God exists behind all natural processes-** "Kena" literally means "by whom". It basically discusses the concept of Brahman and asserts that spirituality and knowledge are the basic longings of all creatures.
3. **KATHA UPANISHAD (YAJUR VEDA)- Immortality is union with God-** The Katha Upanishad is divided into three sections known as Valli. This Upanishad mainly unfolds as a story of a boy named Nachiketa, the son of sage Vajashravas. The boy meets the deity of Death and asks him some questions. Their conversations reveal precious insights about Atman (self), manas (mind) and moksha (liberation).
4. **PRASHNA UPANISHAD (ATHARVA VEDA)- Discourse on Prana-** This Upanishad is in the form of question and answer. A rishi named Pippalada answers six questions of his disciples. The text discusses the nature of Brahman and origin of life.

5. **AITAREYA UPANISHAD (RIG VEDA)- Creation and Pure Consciousness-** This Upanishad unfurls a discussion related to three themes, namely man, Atman and Consciousness. Aitareya Upanishad is thought to have been created before the Creation of the Universe and hence it is considered the oldest of all Upanishads.

6. **TAITTIRIYA UPANISHAD (YAJUR VEDA)- Thou art Brahman-** It is incorporated as three chapters in the Yajurveda. It asserts that the purpose of life is to see Brahman as the omniscient, infinite and the highest truth. "**Atithi Devo Bhava**" comes from this Upanishad.

7. **MUNDAKA UPANISHAD (ATHARVA VEDA)- Knowledge and Wisdom-** This Upanishad is written in the form of mantras. These mantras are used for imparting spiritual knowledge as well as teachings on meditation. The national motto of India "**Satyamev Jayate**" is derived from Mundaka Upanishad.

8. **MANDUKYA UPANISHAD (ATHARVA VEDA)- Meaning of Aum-** This is the shortest of all ten Upanishads. This Upanishad describes the four states of consciousness. Lord Ram in a conversation with Hanuman told him to read Mandukya and he will attain self-realization.

9. **CHANDOGYA UPANISHAD (SAMA VEDA)- Tat Tvam Asi-** This Upanishad discusses the importance of meditation, the power of Om mantra and the significance of Prana, the life force. This Upanishad has the highest number of mantras.

10. BRIHADARANYAKA UPANISHAD (YAJUR VEDA)- Meditation is the way to God- This Upanishad was written by Yajnavalkya. It asserts that the world is more than just matter and energy. It is comprised of Atman or Brahman and Knowledge. It discusses metaphysics and nature of Reality

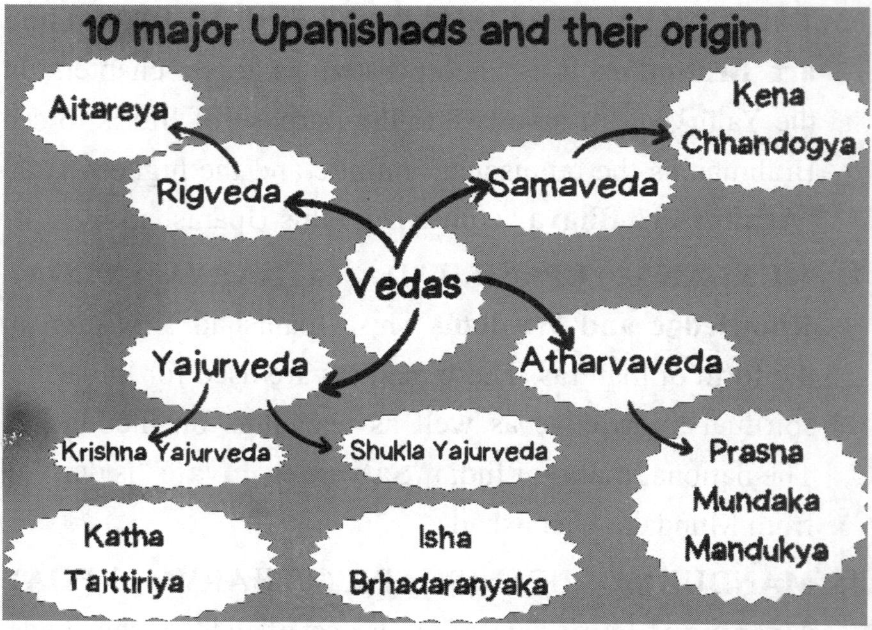

Lesson 1: Discover Yourself - "Tat Tvam Asi" (That Thou Art) (Chandogya Upanishad)

Story 1: *Satyakama Jabala's Search for Brahman*

The first story has been taken from Chandogya Upanishad. The Chandogya Upanishad is one of the most famous and often-read Upanishads. The most important theme in this Upanishad is the significance of chants, speech and song to human salvation and knowledge. This Upanishad also discusses Aum, which is regularly used in the practice of meditative yoga. The Upanishad has eight chapters and it describes many aspects of Hindu philosophy including concepts such as good and evil, space, the universe as a whole, the Soul and Self, oneness with the world and Brahman. It is a poetic text with a metered structure, focusing on song, language and chanting.

This story is about Satyakama Jabala, a young boy, who wanted to find out the nature of Brahman (the Supreme Truth). Here goes the story:

Long ago, in a dense forest, lived a small boy with his mother. The boy's mother named him Satyakama, which meant "seeker of truth" in Sanskrit. The boy was keen to learn meditation and know the nature of the brahman from a guru. He wanted to lead a true shishya's life spent at an ashram practising meditation and learning about Brahman. Nevertheless, in those days, teachers only accepted pupils from specific families. Thus in order to become such a student, he had to be aware of his father's family name. Satyakama informed his mother,

Jabala, that he desired to lead a life as a student of spiritual knowledge. Jabala was happy to know that her child wished to take brahman-vidya.

"Dear Mother, what family do I belong to?" Satyakama further enquired.

His mother addressed him, saying, "My beautiful son, I do not know your family name"

Satyakama inquired sincerely, "So what shall I tell my guru, Mother?"

Her mother, Jabala, who was a poor lady, had lived a virtuous life and recognized the strength of telling the truth. She told him that she was not sure to which lineage he belonged. However, she was Jabala by name and he was Satyakama. She said, "Tell him exactly what I told you, my dear son."

Hearing this, Satyakama embarked on his journey and left his mother's home to begin seeking a guru. He departed from his house with the approval of his mother. For days, he traversed dense jungles on foot before he found the sage Gautama, who resided in an ashram at the edge of the forest.

Satyakama showed respect for the teacher by bowing down and said, "Honoured Sir, would you kindly accept me as your shishya? I hope to learn about Brahman with your blessing."

The boy appeared bright and healthy in Gautama's opinion. Yet Gautama needed to be aware of the boy's family history in order to accept him as a student and most importantly as his disciple. He inquired, "What family do you belong to, dear boy?"

"My mother told me that I should tell you that her name is Jabala and my name is Satyakama—and I know nothing more about my family," the young boy replied bravely. "I am therefore Satyakama Jabala"

Gautama was glad the boy's mother had instilled in him the value of telling the truth. "I will happily welcome you as my pupil," he said. "Only one belonging from the best of families could give this explanation with such sincerity," he thought. Gautama agreed to accept Satyakama as his pupil. Satyakama felt extremely happy. At last, he felt that he would be able to study the knowledge of Brahman.

The following day, the wise Gautama taught Satyakama how to meditate in order to calm his thoughts. Knowing oneself, or having Brahma vidya, is the first step towards discovering Brahman. Satyakama experienced his inner Self after practising deep meditation. It was like a wide ocean of silence building a tender and calm mind to develop his thoughts. After instructing Satyakama in meditation, Gautama took a very uncommon action. He led Satyakama to the grassland, where there were a large number of cows grazing.

Satyakama was shocked as Gautama picked some four hundred skinny cows and informed Satyakama that he would soon embark on a different kind of voyage, a journey of a true knowledge seeker. He asked Satyakama to carefully tend to the cows and take them to another part of the forest and come back when their count increases to a total of thousand cows. Though Satyakama had many concerns in his heart, he left the gurukul with the cows into the deepest part of the forest.

Satyakama led the herd of four hundred cows to a beautiful meadow to the other side of the forest as suggested by his guru and hence began his new life.

While he tended the cows along this journey, he initially experienced loneliness. But soon, he tried to find solace in his cows, making them his family. He tried to make peace with the surrounding nature as well. He soon forgot even the human language he had grown up with. Even the purpose of this journey had vanished from his memory, leaving him in complete silence. While living deep in the forest with a herd of hundred and more cows, he even lost all sense of time. He started to enjoy his time in the jungle. He experienced euphoria, bliss, and delight by becoming one with the nature and by being fully present in the moment. He gave the cows loving attention. His cows were given access to clean stream of water and fresh grass. He saw pleasure in seeing his cows becoming healthy. The cow herd grew bigger as Satyakama grew older.

When they dozed off, he even sang to the cows, who responded to him by mooing. In the woods and among other wild species, Satyakama began to enjoy his life. There was a significant transformation in his personality. He experienced a state of calmness, a love-filled heart, and a radiant smile on his face.

After several years of peaceful living in the forest along with the cows, he was composed in his thoughts as his days began with meditation and finished with it. For several years, Satyakama remained in the dense forest leading a tranquil and contented life. He even forgot his goal of returning to his guru with a thousand cows.

When the time came the wise bull who was the head of the cows, called out to him; "Satyakama!" "We have reached a total count of thousand cows," the bull declared. "Please lead us to the hermitage of your guru... And I'll show you the numerous facets about the nature of Brahman".

"Sure, tell me please," Satyakama responded.

"The bull told him that Brahman shone from north to south as well as from east to west. This is because Brahman permeates all things. It is common knowledge. This represents one-fourth of Brahman."

The bull then remarked, "Agni, the fire will teach you more about Brahman."

While Satyakama took the cows back to ashram, he surrounded a sizeable area with a rope in the evening to keep the cows safe. Next, Satyakama started a fire. He took a seat facing east on the west side of the fire. He looked up at the starry, night sky that was home to his friends. After some time, Agni, the fire, talked to him and explained what a Brahman is.

Agni remarked, "Brahma is the sky and the ocean; it is the ground and the atmosphere. This is due to Brahman's limitless nature. It has neither a start nor a finish. This represents one-fourth of Brahman. A swan will teach you more about Brahman," Agni continued.

Satyakama again started a fire by the side of a river the following evening after travelling back to the ashram with his cows. He saw a big white swan gliding down the river towards him as he sat down, facing east. Satyakama was starting to learn about the nature of Brahman from the swan.

The swan said, "Brahman is fire, and Brahman is the sun. The moon is Brahman, and lightning is Brahman. The life's light is Brahman."

The swan continued, "A bird will explain Brahman to you further."

After locating his cows in a secure location near a hill the following evening, Satyakama started a fire once more. He took a seat on the soft, dry grass and looked east. A purple sunbird descended from a tree branch at this particular time. Its wings reflected the fire's radiance like silk braided with gold.

The sunbird began to sing, "Brahman is the breath, and Brahman is the eye. The ear and the mind are both Brahman.

This section of Brahman serves as a seat and a place to rest. The seat of everything is Brahman, just as the eye and the mind are the seats of what is seen and conceived, respectively. Everything is brahman!" Satyakama finally made it to his teacher's home.

Sage Gautama then referred to the cows as he saw Satyakama and said, "Now one thousand and one cows have returned." In other words, Satyakama himself had completely lost all memory of his previous individuality and had become one with the herd.

"I perceive that you have found Brahman," his teacher told Satyakama as he realized that Satyakama had finally become enlightened and had discovered the true meaning of Brahman and life.

Instead, Satyakama requested his Guru with humility, "Please, Sir, teach me about the nature of Brahman," Satyakama wished to understand the genuine nature of Brahman from his master.

The guru simply said, "**Tat Tvam Asi**," which translates to "**That Thou Art**," the Vedic statement for enlightenment. The words of the guru just entered Satyakama's being and took on actuality in him since he was so devoid of his own identity and in a state of absolute listening. At that time, Satyakama received enlightenment.

His teacher further added, "You have heard that the east and the west are Brahman, the earth and the sky are Brahman, the sun and moon are Brahman, and the sight and the ear are Brahman. All of these are components of Brahman churning like ocean waves. Brahman permeates all things, which explains this. Everything is Brahman. It never ends. The light of life, it is. In Brahman, everything finds rest. The Self, our inner identity, must be known in order to realize Brahman completely. When that happens, you come to understand that you are radiant and limitless, present everywhere. Brahma Vidya, hence is the greatest wisdom."

And in this manner Satyakama learned about Brahman.

Only a guru can create the ideal environment for a disciple to flourish. A disciple, a seeker of knowledge can achieve the level of absolute joy only under the direction and teaching of an enlightened guru. Like all spiritual seekers, Satyakama had his share of doubts, but he was also intelligent enough to pay attention to what his guru had to say and was courageous enough to put the Guru's advice into practice. Satyakama was able to transcend the ordinary realm and enter a higher state of consciousness in this way. A method to reach eternal consciousness happens through the guru. The seeker must possess the fortitude, tenacity, and acumen to make the first move in the right direction.

The probability of attaining enlightenment and experiencing perpetual happiness increases thereafter.

Student Takeaways

The story shows the discipline and perseverance of Satyakama to pursue his quest for ultimate knowledge irrespective of various factors like caste and religion. His story teaches:

1. **Honesty:** Satyakama's honest admission of not knowing his father's identity was crucial in earning Gautama's trust and guidance. That's why it is often said 'Honesty is the best policy'. As a student, you should also follow this mantra. Let's take the example of an exam, even when you are not aware of the answers in any school examination, you should never think of cheating or getting involved in any wrong deed to score well. Be honest, face the situation and you will definitely feel good and satisfied at the end!

2. **Service:** Just like Satyakama's diligent service to the cows a way of learning important virtues, you should also make

it a point to attain these qualities while learning any new activity. For example, if you are learning a new sport in school, you tend to learn many other qualities like leadership, team work, building strategy etc. along with learning that sport. Sports help in building healthy bones and muscles, increases fitness, improves sleep, helps you socialize. It also improves cooperation skills, boosts self-confidence and lowers the risk of getting obese. So, what we see here is that while learning a sport, you pick up so many other things. Follow this principle in all spheres of life.

3. **Determination:** Satyakama's dedication to his studies despite his difficult circumstances and lack of a clear family lineage ultimately led him to achieve his goal of studying the Vedas. Similarly, at all stages of life, you should also follow your heart and stay focused. You may come across many distractions around you. There may be a temptation to watch reels on smartphone or update status on social media, you may feel like enjoying your favourite television show, you may wish to go for a movie or party with friends, there could be many more distractions to take you away from your goal but you should never allow yourself to get lost and wander away from your target.

4. **Enjoy the Journey:** Satyakama's service to the cows was so intense that he completely forgot about his ultimate aim and started to enjoy his new life, so much so that he was reminded of his true ambition by a bull. Thus, as a student, you should also focus on mastering the subject that you are studying and not think about scoring marks and securing ranks.

5. **Finding Solace in Your Own Company:** As young people we often want to be a part of everything and we are scared of missing out. It is important to have a social life but you must not always require somebody's company. Being comfortable with yourself is the first step to independence. **Most of us do not understand the difference between being alone and lonely. One should spend time with oneself (being alone) rather than feel lonely (needing the company of others). Those who can enjoy their own company become much better students.**

Reflection Time

Answer the following questions on how to practically use the teachings in your life.

1. **What was the last act of service you performed without a selfish motive?**

   (You must indulge in some kind of service; it could be as simple as feeding stray animals or being kind to people and helping your friends. When you do your chores at home or work at night, try out the principle of hard work. Go the extra mile and do more than you usually do.)

   ____

   ____

   ____

2. **Do you often get distracted from your goal? If yes, how do you bring your focus back?**

   (Identify one easy task that needs to be done today, like practicing the piano, cleaning room/washing clothes, or finish reading a book for the English assignment. Decide when you will do it. Then keep your word and do it with complete focus.)

   ____

   ____

   ____

3. **Have you ever observed a flow state when you get so deeply engrossed in an activity that you loose track of time? You enjoy the journey so much that you forget about the destination. This happened with Satyakama when he was taking care of the cows.**

____

____

____

4. **How open-minded are you to learn from everyone?** (Satyakam Jabala was taught the knowledge of Brahman not by humans but by birds and beasts. This illustrates how much there is to learn from anyone and everyone.)

____

____

____

5. **How often do you remain true to yourself and act according to your nature? And how often do you pretend to be somebody you are really not?**

   (When sage Gautama asked about his family name, Satyakama could have lied due to fear of being rejected, but he stayed true to himself and conveyed the truth about his birth that his mother had told him.)

____

____

____

6. **Try developing a habit of doing a certain activity every day before you sit down to study.**

   (This habit can be anything. You can try meditating for 5-10 minutes, or chant a small prayer or mantra like the one mentioned below.)

   ____

   ____

   ____

"Om Saha Nau-Avatu |
Saha Nau Bhunaktu |
Saha Viiryam Karavaavahai |
Tejasvi Nau-Adhiitam-Astu Maa Vidvissaavahai |
Om Shaantih Shaantih Shaantih ||"

Lesson 2: Fear Not, Keep Seeking – "What is the secret of death?" (Katha Upanishad)

Story 2: *A Dialogue with the God of Death*

The Katha Upanishad is one of the most popular and most loved Upanishads of all. This is because of its linguistic simplicity and clarity in making the subject matter regarding the highest truth easily comprehensible. It has a total of 120 verses. This Upanishad contains the famous story of Nachiketa, a young, disciplined, intelligent and a sincere boy who attains enlightenment after his meeting with Yama, the God of Death.

Nachiketa was the son of the sage Vajashravas, who wished to perform a sacrificial ritual named Viswajet Yagna. This yagna was a sacred ritual in the Vedic context, where the performer had to give away all the material possessions that he had. This included his wife, children, house and everything that constituted his wealth. In ancient times, cows were also considered as an individual's sacred possession.

Nachiketa was small when his father took such a vow to perform the sacred yagna. As a part of his vow, Nachiketa's father decided to give away all the sick cows, useless property, and all the things he didn't want, which were considered as a burden in one way or another. He made a big show of the sacrifice, but kept everything that he really needed, including his two wives and children. Nachiketa paid close attention to what his father did. He was surprised to notice that his father was giving away only old and disabled cows that were unable to give milk. Nachiketa was pained by this, as he understood that his father will not get the fruits of the yagna since the offering was not right. He confronted his father to tell him what he was actually doing. If he didn't want to give away everything, he shouldn't have taken the vow. He further mentioned that once he had taken the vow and was set on his ultimate goal, he must do it properly, and so he will have to give away everything, including his own son.

Having said this, Nachiketa became curious as to which deity his father would dedicate him to. At first, Vajashravas gave no response. Nachiketa asked the same question again, but all his efforts went in vain as his father tried to do away with his son's quest. However, Nachiketa was persistent and when he asked the same question the third time, Vajashravas could no longer control his temper and, in anger, said, "I am going to give you to Yama. Do you know who he is? Yama, the Lord of Death!" Vajashravas was fuming with anger when he said this, but the poor boy took every word of his father seriously. He decided to go to Yama, as he wanted to complete his father's vow and follow the yagna rituals sincerely, as inscribed in the Vedas.

Following his father's words, Nachiketa reached the kingdom of Yama. However, after reaching the door of Yama's kingdom, Nachiketa realized that the Lord of Death was not present in his abode and would take some days to return. Nachiketa decided to wait for Lord Yama to return. He sat right near the gate and waited for nearly three days and three nights without consuming a drop of water.

When Yama came back, he saw this little boy, Nachiketa, in an absolute state of hunger and exhaustion but full of determination and patience. Yama was moved by the boy's devotion. While waiting for Yama, Nachiketa hadn't even thought of going and looking for food. He was just sitting there and waiting for him.

So, Yama said, "I admire your determination and the patience with which you have been waiting here for the past three days." He continued, "Dear child, you are my guest, the brahman, and I would be glad to serve you. I'll grant you three boons. Tell me, what do you want?"

Nachiketa greeted Lord Yama and acknowledged his generosity in granting him three boons of his choice. He said, "I recognize my mistake as I made my father fume with anger before I came here." He continued, "I am worried that in my absence, he must be upset and concerned about me. Hence, I would like to request you to give my father all that he wants, all the wealth that he needs, and make him happy again so that when I return, he isn't angry anymore," Nachiketa requested Lord Yama with concern in his voice. Lord Yama agreed and granted him the first boon.

The second boon that he asked for was to know about the ritual of fire sacrifice. He wanted to know more about all the karmas enlisted in the Vedas, what kinds of yagnas are required to attain bliss, and how one can achieve them. Yama agreed to elaborate on what he can do to attain the blessing of God through yagnas. Nachiketa carefully listened to everything that the master said and tried to grasp the sacred Vedic knowledge of all yagnas in relation to the ritual of fire sacrifice.

After this, Lord Yama asked him for his last boon, hearing which he was left speechless. On hearing this question, even Lord Yama was unsure about the absolute answer to the question that Nachiketa had asked. What did Nachiketa ask for?

Nachiketa, out of complete innocence, asked him,

"What is the secret of death?"

"What happens after death?"

"Where do we go after we die?"

Lord Yama was not ready to answer this question. He instead tried to persuade the boy to take anything, including all the riches of the world or a particular kingdom that he wished to rule. He could ask for just anything. But nothing worked for Yama. Nachiketa said, "What will I do with all of these riches and pleasures, my lord? You've already told me that all these things are transient and meaningless for human existence. After this, my goal is clearer than ever. I have understood that all these activities and pleasures—everything that people are involved in—are meaningless at the end of the day. I don't want anything else except the answer to this question of mine."

However, Yama was still persistent when it came to persuade the boy to withdraw his question, but nothing worked as the boy was sincere in his quest and Yama was obligated to grant his vow. In many ways, Yama tried to avoid this question. He further added, "No one, not even the gods, knows the answer to this question." "It cannot be given to you." Nachiketa said, "If that is so, and the gods do not know the answer and only you know it, then you must definitely give me the answer."

Yet again, Nachiketa was true to what he sought to take from his quest. He was clear about what he wanted, and just wouldn't give up. So once again, Yama left him there and stayed away from his abode for a few months. He just wanted to avoid this boy somehow. He wanted to get rid of him, but Nachiketa stuck around him for many months. The actual essence of self, stayed on with Nachiketa, and Yama was secretly pleased with the discipline of this little boy. Impressed with his persistence, Yama imparted the knowledge and the true meaning of death.

As it is said, Nachiketa attained enlightenment right on the doorstep of Yama's domain. He got the answers to everything he had to know about the existence of human life and dissolved himself in pursuit of the same. He was the first such seeker of truth, and his example is always used to shine a light on the meaning of how patience leads one towards the path of prosperity and success. He knew what he wanted, and he did everything to get it. That's all there is to it.

When you are like Nachiketa, there is no need for a path for you. It is already here, and you shall carve it further. The only way to move forward is to stay focused on what you started. That is what Nachiketa did. He questioned not only his father but also the god of death. He was fearless, for he knew how to follow one course until he succeeded in reaching the goal.

Thus, if you are committed to your objective your path is very much in front of you. It is your commitment that keeps you moving forward. If there is no intensity, neither practice nor kriya will be effective. And if there is intensity, the practice will transport you to another realm.

It is surprising to see Nachiketa's single-mindedness of purpose. No wonder that Swami Vivekananda, a reformer and great teacher, was too fond of the character of Nachiketa. This great leader found Katha Upanishad "most marvellous" and said "Among the Upanishads, one finds no other book so beautiful as this (Katha). I wish you would all learn it by heart."

Swamiji was so impressed by Nachiketa that he once said, “If I get ten or twelve boys with the faith of Nachiketa, I can turn the thoughts and pursuits of this country in a new channel.” This statement of Swami Vivekananda is a perfect example that proves that single minded determination produces the desired result in helping one to achieve his/her goal.

Student Takeaways

Be fearless in pursuit of knowledge. When your path is defined, know that no one can stop you not even the god of death. It’s interesting to note that the main protagonist in the Katha Upanishad is not a wise sage or god, but a teenager. A few lessons from this story are as follows-

1. **Curiosity:** Nachiketa’s determination to seek answers to his questions demonstrates the importance of asking questions and seeking answers. As a student, it is essential for you to never let your curiosity fade. You should ask questions to gain a deeper understanding of the world around you. Do remember, to be successful in life, never keep any doubts. This is the reason why teachers also encourage students to ask questions. Always ask your doubts in class.
2. **Persistence:** Nachiketa’s persistence in seeking knowledge despite facing obstacles and setbacks is a lesson for all students. It is crucial to persist in your pursuit of knowledge, even when faced with challenges and difficulties. The key of persistence opens all doors in life. So, no matter what the situation is, continue learning whatever you want to, it may be a new language, a new activity, a new game or a new subject.

3. Understanding: Nachiketa's ability to distinguish and understand the difference between the superficial and the essential, and to choose the latter, is a great mark of distinction and students should try to develop this crucial quality. It is essential to focus on the important aspects that will help you learn and grow. So, learn to choose what is good for you. There may be a situation where you may be required to choose between going out for a party and studying for your approaching exams. Think wisely, understand and choose that which will help you in life.

4. Mentor: Nachiketa's journey highlights the importance of having a mentor or teacher who can guide us on our path to knowledge. A good mentor can help you navigate the complexities of learning and provide valuable guidance and support. Without teachers, it may be difficult for you to succeed. Teachers play a major role in the success of many people.

5. Beliefs: Whatever you do, do it with 100% commitment. Nachiketa's determination to know about the fundamental truths about death was such, that he ended up at the doorsteps of Yamraj and finally with persistent efforts was enlightened. Similarly, whenever you choose any goal, do it with 100% commitment. Remember that half-hearted efforts don't give half results; they give zero results.

Reflection Time

Answer the following questions to practically use the learnings from the story in your life.

1. **Are you a curious person who always likes to explore things?**

   (Whenever you are curious about anything try finding answers and learn new things. In order to keep growing in life, it is important that you stay inquisitive.)

   ____

   ____

   ____

2. **If you could spend an hour with any person who ever lived, who would that be? Why did you choose this person? What would you ask them?**

   (This person could be anyone from history. Look up information about this person and what is it that they inspire in you. Reading about great personalities and their life helps you identify and align your interests and goals.)

   ____

   ____

   ____

3. How do you practice the virtue of "Loyalty" in your life?

(Pinpoint when and where it's most difficult for you to hold back from gossiping. Is it with a certain friend, in the locker room, on social media? Come up with a plan of action to avoid doing it. Try to go one whole week saying only positive things about others online .You can try to organize a "positive social media attack." It's simple! Get your friends to attack someone with kind words and compliments on their social media photos and posts.)

____

____

____

4. How determined are you to achieve your goals?

(Despite having presented with every possible treasure by the God of Death, Nachiketa wasn't distracted or wavered from his quest and remained single-minded and persistent in seeking the answers to his questions. How persistent are you?)

____

____

____

5. **As you noticed, this Upanishad revolves around Nachiketa, a teenager. What qualities you liked about Nachiketa? How can you become like Nachiketa?** (Be courageous. Don't hesitate to ask questions; get out of your comfort zone; question traditions, cultures, beliefs respectfully. Ask for explanation if you are not convinced. Don't accept anything blindly.)

____

____

____

Lesson 3: Be Mindful – "Rejoice in the Self" (Chandogya Upanishad)

***Story 3:** From Darkness to Light*

The next story is from the Chandogya Upanishad, which belongs to Sama Veda. It's a big Upanishad consisting of 8 chapters and 627 mantras. In fact, among the 10 Principal Upanishads, Chandogya has the highest number of mantras.

The story is about Narada, a Vedic sage, famous in Hindu traditions as a travelling musician and storyteller and a great Bhakta of Lord Vishnu, who looks for 'Self' beyond sorrow.

Once Narada approached the sage Sanatkumara and requested him to show him the path of knowledge and teach him about the highest truth.

"Tell me what you know, and then I will teach you what is beyond that," thus said Sanatkumara to Narada.

Then Narada told him with all humility, "Sir, I have read the Rig Veda, the Yajur Veda, the Sāma Veda, and the Atharva Veda; I have read the Puranas; also, grammar, funeral rites, mathematics, the science of omens, the science of underground resources, logic, moral science, astrology, Vedic knowledge, the science of the elements, archery, astronomy, the science relating to snakes, plus music, dance, and other fine arts. Sir, this is what I know. But I know only the meaning of the word. All this knowledge has not helped me to know the Self. I have heard from spiritual teachers like you that one who realizes the Self goes beyond sorrow. I am lost in sorrow. Please teach me how to go beyond it."

There is a very long dialogue between Narada and Sanatkumar after which Sanatkumar reveals to Narada that speech is greater than name, mind is greater than speech, will is greater than mind, consciousness is greater than will, meditation is greater than consciousness, understanding is greater than meditation, power is greater than understanding, food is greater than power, water is greater than food, fire is greater than water, space is greater than water and Atman or the Spirit is greater than fire and is the substratum of everything else. Man is always impelled to do things on account of joy or the pleasure that he gets out of the things that he does. No one acts or does anything unless motivated by some kind of pleasure or joy. But it is the Infinite that is the source of abiding joy because it is not subject to change. Therefore, one must seek to know the Infinite.

With this, Sanatkumar taught Narada the nature of the Infinite. "Where one realizes the indivisible unity of life, sees nothing else, hears nothing else, knows nothing else, that is the Infinite. The Infinite is beyond death, but the finite cannot escape death."

Sanatkumar also shared, "Dear Narada, the Infinite depends on its own glory, no not even that. In the world, people think they can attain glory by having cows and horses, elephants and gold, family and servants, fields and mansions. But I do not call that glory, for here one thing depends on another. But the Infinite is utterly independent. The Infinite is above and below, before and behind, to the right and to the left. I am all this. The Self is above and below, before and behind, to the right and to the left. I am all this. One who meditates on the Self and realizes the Self, sees the Self everywhere, and rejoices in the Self. Such a person lives in freedom and is at home wherever he goes. He discovers that everything in the cosmos – energy and space, fire and water, names and forms, birth and death, mind and will, word and deed, mantra and meditation – all come from the Self. He goes beyond decay and death, beyond separateness and sorrow. But those who pursue the finite are blind to the Self and live in bondage. Therefore, O Narada, control the senses and purify the mind. In a pure mind there is a constant awareness of the Self. Where there is constant awareness of the self, freedom ends bondage and joy ends sorrow."

Thus, the sage Sanatkumar taught the pure Narada to go beyond bondage, beyond sorrow, beyond darkness, to the light of the Self. He taught Narada, who was pure in heart, how to pass from darkness into light.

Student Takeaways

The story of Narada and Sanatkumara teaches us some important lessons. A few learnings from this story:

1. **Always be a learner:** The story emphasizes the importance of humility and the recognition of one's limitations. Narada, who was initially confident in his knowledge, realized his ignorance and was quite humble to ask for guidance. This makes it evident that every person is a learner throughout life. So, be aware! If you feel that you are not knowledgeable about a particular topic, chapter, game, activity or anything, become a student and gain knowledge of that particular subject. Never be overconfident in life.

2. **The Principle of Pleasure:** The Vedas speak about two kinds of pleasure: Shreya and Preya. Shreya is that pleasure which seems bitter in the beginning but becomes very sweet in the long run. Preya is that pleasure which seems pleasant in the present but causes great pain later. The difference between them is akin to delayed gratification versus immediate gratification. An example of Shreya is the eating of amla or the Indian gooseberry. Amla is a super food that is very beneficial for health. Each amla has the vitamin C of ten oranges. However, children dislike it since it has a bitter taste.

3. **Importance of a Teacher:** Sanatkumara, the sage and a teacher to Narada, played a crucial role in guiding him towards

the ultimate truth. Without the support of Sanatkumara, it would not have been possible for Narada to attain what he wished to. He would not have walked on the path of self-realization without a mentor. Do you remember the date 5th September, the day when we celebrate Teachers' Day across India? It is a day to show gratitude towards the person who patiently hears you every time when you ask a question. It is a tribute to the contribution made by teachers to the society. Remember to respect your teachers and be thankful to them.

4. Meditation and Self-realization: Sanatkumara taught Narada the importance of meditation and self-realization in attaining true knowledge and understanding of the nature of reality. For a student, meditation could be complete dedication towards a particular goal. The actual act of meditation is to build concentration on an object or sound for a few minutes. If you are able to do that even for a couple of minutes, it may help boost your focus and concentration for longer periods while studying. You may even be able to complete tasks or solve math problems with greater ease.

Reflection Time

Answer the following questions to practically use the teachings in your life.

1. **Look in the mirror and ask, "Would I want to spend time with someone like me?"**

   (If the answer to this question is no, work to develop the qualities that you think you're lacking)

   ____

   ____

   ____

2. **Do you feel distracted and anxious when trying to focus on a topic?**

   (Excessive use of social media and smart phones makes students anxious. In order to cope with this anxiety, you should try yoga. It is a good way to balance the mind and the body.)

   ____

   ____

   ____

3. **Do you think there is a difference between worrying and thinking?**

   (Often we worry about things, be it studying, future or any goals. You must realize that worrying won't get you anywhere but thinking is the first step to planning. When you think about a problem, the solution to it is right around the corner. Worrying will not help you solve any problem.)

____

____

____

4. **What do you think are your strengths and weakness?**

   (Use your tool of self-awareness right now by asking yourself, "What is my most unhealthy habit?" Make up your mind to do something about it.)

   Most unhealthy habit: ________________________

   What I'm going to do about it: __________________

   ____

   ____

   ____

5. **How much time do you dedicate to acquiring self-knowledge?**

   (Despite being knowledgeable about a wide array of subjects, Narada was deeply drenched in sorrow. This displays how only the right kind of knowledge dispels the inner ignorance and shines the light of consciousness within our hearts. You may be knowledgeable in various subjects, but how knowledgeable are you about yourself?)

   ____

   ____

   ____

Lesson 4: Belief in the Self Brings Success – "the subtle essence, it is here" (Chandogya Upanishad)

Story 4: *Uddalaka Rishi and his disciple-son, Shvetaketu*

The crux of the Chandogya Upanishad is the famous Mahavakya- 'Tat Tvam Asi'. Here, the Upanishad presents Brahma Vidya (the knowledge of the Supreme Truth) in form of a dialogue, as a discussion between the Guru-father, Uddalaka Rishi and his disciple-son, Shvetaketu. In this Upanishad, the central teaching - the oneness between the individual and the Supreme Truth - is imparted by striking similes and apt metaphors.

This story revolves around Shvetketu, who undergoes the journey from ignorance to knowledge of the self and truth.

Uddalaka was a great rishi. He had a son by name Svetaketu. When Svetaketu turned twelve, Uddalaka asked him to go and get his education from a Gurukula. As directed by his father, Svetaketu went to a Gurukula and studied the Vedas under the guru. He returned home when he was twenty-four years of age as a proud scholar. He thought that there remained little for him to know. When he returned from the Gurukula his father Uddalaka noticed arrogance in his expression. He wanted to teach him a lesson in humility.

So, Uddalaka called him by his side and asked him, "Svetaketu, my boy, have you, ever sought out the knowledge of that by which the unheard can be heard, the unseen can be seen, and the unknowable can be known?" Svetaketu was surprised. He had no idea about what his father had asked. Therefore, he requested his father to give him this knowledge.

Uddalaka told Svetaketu, "Son, by knowing one lump of clay you may learn about everything made of clay; the only difference between such things is the name, a result of speech. But the truth is that all such things are of the same substance. Likewise, by knowing one chunk of gold, you may learn about everything made of gold; the only difference between such things is the name, a result of speech. But the truth is that all such things are of the same substance. And the same is true for even the simplest tools made of iron. This, my son, is the knowledge of what I speak."

Uddalaka continued, "Dear child, in the beginning of things there was pure being, one without a second. It wanted to become many. Then, it manifested itself in the form of fire and from fire came water and from there came food. This way a rich variety of things came into existence by permutation and combination of these forms. Then life appeared, and among the living beings there came man with his varied powers and functions."

Svetaketu stopped his father from going ahead and asked him to explain what a man would do during sleep.

Uddalaka explained, "The man becomes one with the Spirit, the eternal Being. Man's mind is like a beast tied to a pole by a long rope. It turns round and round and cannot get away. When a man dies, his power of speech is merged into his mind, his mind is absorbed in the Prana, the Prana is merged into the light, and the light merges in the power beyond. That power is subtle. It pervades the universe. That is the Truth. That is the Spirit. That Thou art, O Svetaketu."

However, this did not satisfy Svetaketu. He wanted to know more about that all pervading power. So, Uddalaka said, "Dear child, bees bring droplets of honey from various flowers and store in the hive. Once in the hive, do the droplets know from which flower they came? Do they need to know it? So, too all these beings when merge into the ocean of Being, they know not from where they came. All become one when they have merged in the ocean of consciousness, of the One Being. That is subtle. That pervades everything. That is the Atman. That thou art, O Svetaketu."

Then Uddalaka gave another example of all rivers merging into the ocean and losing their individual identity. Then he shared an example in which he explained that by cutting a part of the tree the whole tree does not die. Only that part which is cut dies. Thus, that which is deprived of its life dies but the life itself does not die. The power by which life lives eternally is the Spirit. That thou art O Svetaketu."

Svetaketu listened to his father attentively and said: "My respected teachers must not have known this, for if they had, they surely would have told me. Won't you please give me more of this knowledge, Father?" And Uddalaka agreed to do so.

Uddalaka said, "Bring me a fruit from the banyan tree." Shvetaketu brought one. Uddalaka told him to break it open.

Svetaketu did the same. Then, Uddalaka asked him, "What do you see there?" Svetaketu replied, "These tiny seeds."Uddalaka said, "Now break one of them open." Svetaketu obeyed the order. Uddalaka: "What do you see there?" Svetaketu: "Nothing, Father."

Uddalaka said, "My son, you know there is a subtle essence which you do not perceive, but through that essence the truly immense banyan tree exists. Believe it, my son. **Everything that exists has its Self in that subtle essence. It is Truth. It is the Self, and you, Svetaketu, are that (tat tvam asi)**."

Svetaketu further pleaded with his father to teach him more, and Uddalaka continued:

Uddalaka asked his son to bring some salt and put it into a cup of water and bring the cup next morning.

Svetaketu did so. Uddalaka: "You put the salt into the water in this cup. Will you take the salt out?

Svetaketu "I am unable to find the salt; for it has dissolved."

Uddalaka "Taste a drop from the surface of this water. Svetaketu, it is salty."

Uddalaka "Now taste a drop from the middle of the cup."

Svetaketu "It tastes the same, salty."

Uddalaka: "Now taste a drop from the bottom."

Svetaketu "It is salty all the same."

Uddalaka "Now child, you do not see the salt, although it is certainly in the water. Even so, the True Being is present everywhere in this universe, although you do not see Him. He is the essence of all, and the desired of all. He is known to the subtlest intellect."

Svetaketu became humble thereafter, and became a great rishi himself in course of time. Uddalaka: "Likewise, though you cannot hear or perceive or know the subtle essence, it is here. Everything that exists has its Self in that subtle essence. It is Truth. It is the Self, and you, Svetaketu.

Student Takeaways

The story of Svetaketu and Uddalaka teaches us the importance of humility and the pursuit of knowledge and understanding beyond what one already knows. It is a reminder that there is always more to learn and explore in the world around us. Let's put the teachings in points:

1. Be Modest: Svetaketu's arrogance caused him to underestimate the true nature of reality. By contrast, it was his father's humble and patient approach that allowed him to see the deeper truth. As a student, it is important to remain humble and open-minded, recognizing that there is always more to learn. So, in everyday life, if you do not understand anything, do not hesitate to ask. Do it with a pleasing attitude and clear your doubts. Be it academics, sports, or any activity, try to work towards learning. This will help you to come out as a winner in all situations.

2. **Seek Deeper Knowledge:** The story encourages us to seek deeper knowledge and understand beyond what we already know. The path to deep knowledge or developing mastery is not easy. It is like launching a rocket into space. In the first few minutes of the flight as the rocket breaks through the downward pull of gravity, maximum fuel is needed. Once the escape velocity has been achieved, the energy consumed becomes marginal, and the rocket is practically propelled by its own momentum. Hence, more fuel is consumed in the lift-off than in the millions of miles of travel that follows. The same applies to the path of deep knowledge. They exert a gravitational force on our existing knowledge that must be broken with patience, commitment, and understanding. As a student, you should strive to expand your knowledge and explore new ideas and perspectives. If you are keen to know, go beyond the syllabus, explore topics you love. It is quite possible that you may get to know a lot more than your friends and co-students. The famous quote "The more you know, the more you realize how less you know" may seem apt to you. Interesting it would be, isn't it?

3. **Knowledge is Not Enough:** Svetaketu's knowledge of the Vedas was impressive, but it wasn't enough to give him a full understanding of reality. Similarly, as a student, it's important to remember that knowledge alone is not enough. Let's say your physics teacher has taught a concept, you have understood the concept but you do not know how it is applicable in life. So, what is the use of knowing that? 'Nothing', is the simple answer. To make the concept useful, you need to analyse the concept, think critically, reflect and inquire to truly understand the concept. Same goes for the world around you–try and become more self-aware, understand your mental process and develop foresight. Do remember, knowledge without application or vice versa is of no use.

Thus, the story tells us that as students, we should be humble, curious, and open-minded learners who are willing to seek deep understanding of the world around us.

Reflection Time

Answer the following questions to practically use the teachings in your life.

1. **What does modesty mean to you?**

   (Being modest about your flaws and shortcomings is important to grow in life. When you accept your weaknesses, there is a bigger scope of learning those things.)

   ____

   ____

   ____

2. **How do you think you can get one step ahead of others?**

   (In order to stay ahead in life, you must concentrate on acquiring knowledge at a deeper level. Merely learning facts will not lead you anywhere, it is the application of knowledge that you must focus on.)

   ____

   ____

   ____

3. **List 10 things you love to do.**

   (It could be anything–web designing, dance, freestyle rapping, Pinterest browsing, eating ethnic foods, singing . . . anything you absolutely love to do! Now try to pick up a couple of hobbies from this list and do them at least once a week. This is an easy way to find your interests.)

4. **What percentage of your day do you dedicate to self-studying?**

(The importance of self-study was emphasized even in the Upanishads. In the Taitariya Upanishad, the value of self-study is stressed by our Rishis. There is a chapter where the students are given the final instructions during their convocation ceremony. The instructions given was:

'Swadhaya Pravachane Cha'

It means that the students must continue to learn and engage in self studying/learning. It is the daily duty of a student to continue doing self-study (Swadhaya) and also teaching others (Pravachan) on a daily basis).

Lesson 5: Let Compassion be your Strength – "Da! Da! Da!" (Brihadaranyaka Upanishad)

Story 5: *Disciplines of Spiritual Progress*

Okay, so now we come to the shortest and probably the simplest story. It is taken from the Brihadaranyaka Upanishad, which is one of the oldest Upanishad scriptures. It is tenth among the most important 108 Upanishads. Composed in prose, the Brihadaranyaka Upanishad focuses on the nature of reality and the identity of the Self or Atman.

Here, Prajapati, who was the supreme deity in the Vedic period of Hinduism, talks about spiritual growth.

Once all the three creations of Prajapati - the gods, the men, and the demons - went to him. At first, it was the gods who approached Prajapati and said, "Teach us, Sir! What advice do you have for us?"

In reply, Prajapati, the supreme Father uttered only one syllable, 'Da.' Then he said, "Have you understood?"

They answered, "Yes, we have understood. You said, Damayata, which refers to have self-control. You are telling us to exercise self-restraint."

"Yes," agreed Prajapati, "You have understood."

Then the men or humans went to Prajapati and said, "Teach us, Sir."

Prajapati uttered the same syllable, 'Da.' Then he asked the men, "Have you understood?"

They answered, "Yes, we have understood. You said to us, Datta, which means be charitable. You are asking us to give, and give generously."

"Yes," agreed Prajapati, "You have understood."

Finally, came the demons. They also requested Prajapati to teach them ways to achieve spritual growth.

Prajapati uttered the same syllable, 'Da.' Then he said, "Have you understood?"

They said, "Yes, we have understood. You told us Dayadhvam– You are telling us to be compassionate."

"Yes," agreed Prajapati, "You have understood."

Every time the storm cloud thunders it says 'Da! Da! Da!' and that reminds us to be self-controlled, to be charitable and to be compassionate.

For the divine part in each individual, the law given by Prajapati is to be self-controlled. Without self-control one gets caught up by the splendours and riches and becomes egoistic. For the human part in each individual the law given is to be charitable, be generous and self-giving. Without this, one feels completely caught up by one's limitedness. For the demonic part in each individual the law given is to be compassionate. Without this one becomes the slayer of oneself. **So, according to Prajapati, self-control, self-giving and compassion are the three essential components of spiritual progress.**

Student Takeaways

The story tells us that we should always work towards gaining knowledge. The thought that we have learnt everything should never come to our minds. We should always remain a student and never think ourselves to be a teacher. As a student, here are some of the lessons to be remembered:

1. **Seek Knowledge:** In the story, the gods, men, and demons all approach Prajapati with the desire to seek knowledge. Thus, you should seek knowledge and wisdom in your own lives. Do you ever try to get your doubts cleared from your teachers? Chances are that you do not do that. Either you hesitate or you are not interested. You should not do that. You need to take a step forward to gain knowledge. Be open and take the help of your teachers, it is the only mantra to fly high in life.

2. **Teacher as a Guide:** Prajapati acts as a teacher to the gods, men, and demons and guides them on the path to enlightenment. This determines the importance of a knowledgeable and compassionate teacher to help us in our own quest for knowledge. Have you ever thought how difficult it is to understand things without a guide? A student who has a keen interest in stars and planets loves to sit and discuss the cosmos with an astronomy expert. She/he simply enjoys that. This is because of the knowledge and guidance that he gets from that teacher. So, acknowledge the importance of a teacher in your life.

3. **Path to Enlightenment:** The story emphasizes the importance of disciplined practice and self-discipline in the pursuit of spiritual growth. Prajapati instructs the gods, men, and demons to engage in various practices, such as meditation and self-control, in order to attain enlightenment.

4. **Building Discipline:** We develop self control by exercising it, in much the same way as we build our muscles. Every time we follow through on a resolution, we liberate the force of willpower within. In this way, small moment-to-moment victories lead to larger successes. The more we exert our willpower, the greater it grows. But if we neglect it, our self-discipline will dwindle and wither away, like unused muscles in the body. Let us exert ourselves courageously to fight the gravitational pull of our bad habits. Once the new habits begin to grow, it becomes progressively easier, and then, one day the desired behaviour comes naturally.

Overall, this story explains us the importance of seeking knowledge, the role of a teacher in our lives and the path to enlightenment.

Reflection Time

Answer the following questions to practically use the teachings in your life.

1. **Are you scared of approaching teachers with your doubts?**

   (Students often hesitate in asking questions in the classroom. The reasons may be low self-esteem or just the fear of appearing stupid among fellow students. Do remember that a teacher is there for your support and guidance. You must be confident to ask anything.)

   ____

   ____

   ____

2. **If you could spend one day in a library studying anything you wanted. What would it be?**

   (You can think about the kind of books that you truly enjoy reading. Try exploring various genres and developing a reading habit.)

   ____

   ____

   ____

3. Would you describe yourself as a disciplined person?

(Discipline is important if you want to be successful in life. Be it academics, sports or business, all successful people are highly disciplined. It is a value that you should strive for.)

____

____

____

4. List any act of kindness you have done in last week.

(Buy a sandwich for a homeless person this week or handwrite a thank-you note to someone you've wanted to thank for a long time. You can also do a random act of kindness like taking out the trash, fixing your mom's laptop, or making someone's bed.)

____

____

____

Lesson 6: Guru reveals the Brahman to us – "He is the beautiful One, he is the Luminous One" (Chandogya Upanishad)

Story 6: *Upakosala and sage Satyakama Jabala*

Moving on to the next story, this is related to Upakosala, who was a disciple of the sage Satyakama Jabala. The story is from the Chandogya Upanishad, which is a very comprehensive work and covers topics like various forms of worship and meditation, the theory of creation, the path to liberation etc. The range of topics makes the Chandogya Upanishad interesting and complete.

Upakosala lived as a Brahmachari and studied under Satyakama Jabala for 12 years in his Gurukula. After the studies, when Upakosala thought that it was time to leave the Ashram, Satyakama detained him permitting others to depart. Upakosala became sad at his Guru's decision, but he was left with no choice. He continued to stay in the Gurukula and kept doing the work expected of him. He stayed there to think, meditate, and contemplate.

Both Upakosala and Satyakama's wife did not understand why he was detained back by the Guru. Satyakama's wife even tried to plead with him to leave Upakosala so that he could return to his house. She had observed him for twelve long years and knew that he had performed brilliantly as a student and attained sacred knowledge. She tried to convince Satyakaama to let Upakosala go home, but in vain. Satyakama refused and he went on a journey. Satyakama's wife was a kind-hearted lady. She felt sad for Upakosala but could not go against her husband. She offered Upakosala some food to eat with a loving heart. But the heartbroken student was so sad that he did not eat the food. He did not receive it as he was sick at heart. Finally, he broke out and said, "O mother, my heart is still impure; I am too unhappy to eat."

The reason behind Satyakama's decision was that he knew that Upakosala had not yet learned all that was necessary for him and was not ready to lead the life of a householder as per dharma. Upakosala too was aware that his detention was not due to poor academic performance, but rather due to insufficient spiritual knowledge. He kept saying to Satyakama's wife that in him there were many desires which tend towards many things and his mind was preoccupied with such cravings. Upakosala understood that the desires may not be negative or foolish, yet they pull one in many directions, whirling one around and confusing one's mind and consuming all of one's life energies. Only when the mind is fixed on the One can the many be safely attended to. Upakosala kept aspiring for attaining this oneness with the Absolute One.

One day while performing a fire sacrament, Upakosala heard the voice of Agni Deva saying, "This life is Brahman, the sky is Brahman, bliss is Brahman, and know thou Brahman!"

To this Upakosala replied, "I know that life is Brahman, but that the sky is Brahman or that bliss is Brahman I do not know."

He heard the voice again from the fire, "Both," said it, "refers to Brahman" "Earth, food, fire, sun–all these that you worship–are forms of Brahman. He, who is seen in the sun–that one is me. He, who dwells in the east, in the north, in the west, and in the south, he who dwells in the moon, in the stars, and in water–that one is me. He, who dwells in the sky and makes the lightning his home–that one also is me. Know well the true nature of the world that it may never do you harm."

Since the fire is only the manifestation of the Lord himself, the truth was revealed in the form of the fire. The earth, life, the sun, the moon, the stars, the lightening, everything was transformed for Upakosala and he started to deify everything.

There upon the fire, which had been only an earthly fire with which we prepare sacrifices, assumed a new aspect and became the Lord himself. The earth was transformed; life was transformed; the sun, the moon, the stars, the lightning–everything was transformed, and deified. And, thus, the true nature of all things was revealed to Upakosala.

In due time Satyakama returned home. When he saw Upakosala, he said, "My son, your face shines like one who knows Brahman. Who has taught you?" "Beings other than men" replied Upakosala. Then said Satyakama, "My son, what you have learned is true. True also is this which I now teach you. To him who knows it shall no evil cling, even as drops of water cling not to the leaf of the lotus. He who glows in the depths of your eyes– that is Brahman; that is the Self of yourself. He is the Beautiful One, he is the Luminous One. In all the worlds, forever and ever, he shines!"

Thus saying, Satyakama explained to Upakosala more about the Brahman and finally declared him as his worthy disciple.

Student Takeaways

The story tells us that we should always be dedicated towards learning. It also teaches us that we should have complete faith on our guru or mentor. As a student, here are some of the lessons to be remembered:

1. **Thirst to Know:** In the story, Upakosala was keen to gain knowledge. Thus, the story emphasizes as the importance of having a strong desire to know. As a student, you should have a deep desire to learn about the nature of reality. You should not give up until you get what you want.

2. **Importance of a Good Teacher:** A right mentor or teacher can guide you on the path of knowledge. So, have complete belief in your teacher. Suppose you want to learn tennis, then look for a guide who is expert in the game, appreciate his knowledge, learn the tricks from him/her and practice. This may be the only way to learn and grow.

3. **Being Obedient and Respectful:** Upakosala showed great respect for his teacher and was obedient to his instructions, which helped him to gain knowledge and wisdom. Just like Upakosala, you should also listen to your teachers. You should show respect towards them. This builds a feeling of trust, safety and wellbeing. When you respect, you are able to accomplish more together than alone, even if the other person comes from a different background. Misbehaving students often hurt their elders and this slows down their progress in life.

4. Learning as a Process: Studying is a long process. It involves understanding the material being taught to you by your teacher, then working on the material on your own and finally clearing your doubts if any arise. After you read the textbooks and listen to the teacher on the subject, you have enough food for thought. You then need to develop your own ideas based on the lessons from the book and the explanations provided by the teachers. It is like a cow eating grass. First it will gather the grass from the fields in its mouth, but chew on later slowly. This cud-chewing practice gives the cows maximum benefit of their food before it is swallowed.

Similarly, one needs to chew and reflect on the scriptures and the words of the teacher again and again, only after which the knowledge gained gets properly absorbed into our system. We internalize the knowledge completely.

Overall, the story of Upakosala teaches us the importance of having a strong desire for knowledge, finding a good teacher and being dutiful.

Reflection Time

Answer the following questions to practically use the teachings in your life.

1. **Do you think character and competence go hand in hand? If yes, how?**

   (Studies and subject knowledge will help in building competence whereas activities like helping in household chores helps in building character. Character lays the foundation on which competence stands. Competence without character is of no use.)

   ____

   ____

   ____

2. **Do you like to explore and learn things that are not a part of your syllabus?**

   (Knowledge is not limited to your syllabus but encompasses your hobbies as well.)

   ____

   ____

   ____

3. **Who do you look up to for support?**

   (It is essential to have a constant source of support in your life. You can look up to your parents and teachers for that support and encouragement.)

____

____

____

4. **When you offend or hurt someone, are you keen to apologise?**

(Before you go to bed tonight, write a simple message of apology to someone you may have offended.)

____

____

____

5. **How often do you think you just passively hear things instead of listening to them?**

(Take it easy and don't talk so much today. Spend the day listening. Think of a family member you've never really taken the time to listen to, like your mom, your big brother, or grandpa. Take the time.)

____

____

____

Lesson 7: Humility and Knowledge Go Hand in Hand – "Have neither pride nor vanity" (Chandogya Upanishad)

***Story** 7: Raikva- The Cart Driver*

Another interesting and inspirational story from the Chandogya Upanishad is about Raikva, a cart puller by profession but a learned man. This Chandogya Upanishad story is notable for stating the idea of unity of the universe, of realization of this unity within man, and that there is unity and oneness in all beings. The story aptly describes this essence of the Chandogya Upanishad.

Long ago, there was a king called Janashruti, who was not only knowledgeable but also pious and charitable. He even cooked food for all in his kingdom. He considered himself to be the greatest patron and believed that there was no one else like him. He measured his merit by the number of gifts and money he distributed. He had also mastered the languages of birds and beasts.

One night while he was lying in the upper storey of his palace, he saw two swans flying past, all the time conversing with each other. One of them said, "Don't you see the bright band of light that proceeds from the King Janashruti? Beware lest you cross the flaming light of his fame and get yourself burnt. You must know that today there is none as famous as he for abundant charities." Swift came a reaction from the other swan.

"Goodness gracious! You speak as if this Janashruti was greater than Raikva, the cart-puller!

The king is but mad after name and fame. It is this that drives him to action. With all his charities he is ever restless. He hankers after praise." The first swan was taken aback and asked: "Who is this Raikva who is just a cart puller yet is greater than the great Janashruti?"

The king overheard the two swans as they flew out of sight and night closed in on the city. But the king became restless. Raikva's name began to haunt him. "I must find this man little known to fame but one who is at peace with himself and with the world," he decided.

The king Janashruti then dispatched a servant to find the great-soul. It was not an easy task, but with lot of difficulty the servant found Raikva who was scratching himself under a cart. The servant asked him whether he was Raikva. "Yes, I am," was the quiet and dignified reply. The servant went back to the palace and reported to Janashruti.

Janashruti made elaborate preparations and went to Raikva. He took six hundred cows, a chain of gold and a mule-driven carriage for Raikva. He offered them all at the feet of Raikva and said, "Sir, be pleased to accept all this and teach me spiritual knowledge." Raikva's snapped back, "Take back the chain and the carriage and the cows! Knowledge of the Self is not for sale!" Janashruti went back and returned after a while, this time with a thousand cows, a chain of gold, a mule-driven carriage and his own daughter to be offered as wife. He offered all this and prayed that he may be taught the higher truths of existence. Raikva was not moved by the gifts but he was impressed with Janashruti's persistence and sincerity. He thought one who has these two virtues is eminently suited to be a perfect disciple.

Raikva said to the king, "In this creation there are many elements which are worshipped as gods. There is the wind that sweeps everything. The fire burns up whatever comes in contact with it. There is also the vital breath which activates a living being. But all these are moved by the Spirit within. This Spirit is not created by anyone. It exists by itself. And yet it creates and sustains the creation. Thus, the entire creation is a complex instrument that is carrying out its work at the behest of the Spirit."

Raikva added, "O king! Have neither pride nor vanity for the charities that you dispense. Go thou, great king, to thy palace. Give but not with pride. Give generously but not with egotism. Give freely but not with an eye to fame. Give but not as something that is yours, but as something given to you by the Spirit for giving to others. He who sees this truth becomes a seer and to him nothing is wanting and he becomes the enjoyer of things."

The king felt satisfied with these words of Raikva. He understood the essence of what Raikva wanted to say. While departing, the king gave a thousand milch cattle, numerous gold coins and chariots, and his own daughter in marriage to Raikva. After this incident, the village came to be known as Raikvaparna village, currently located near Rameswaram in the southern India.

The Vedic scriptures describe our antahkaran (mind or ethereal heart) as having four aspects:

1. **Mind(Mana) :** It creates the thoughts, feelings, desires, hankerings, and aversions.

2. **Intellect(Buddhi) :** Its function is to analyse and decide. It understands, decides, and discriminates i.e. this is good, this is bad.

3. **Subconscious Mind(Chitta) :** It is the storehouse of impressions and memories. It enables one to get attached to an object or person.

4. **Ego(Ahankar) :** It is the ego or 'I'ness. It produces the sense of identity with the attributes of the body and creates pride.

So be careful about your ego!

Student Takeaways

The most important thing that this story teaches us is to be humble. As a student, here are some of the lessons to be remembered:

1. **Being Calm:** The story emphasizes the importance of calmness and humility. Raikva, despite being just a cart driver, possessed great knowledge and wisdom, but he was humble and did not seek recognition or status for his knowledge. In fact, he was ready to share his knowledge freely with those who were willing to learn from him. To put it simply, if you help someone in any manner and boast about it, then your gesture loses its meaning. It becomes useless to you.

2. Importance of Perseverance: King Janashruti was keen to learn and it was his persistent and sincere efforts that took him towards his goal. So, one should continuously work towards his/her target. You should be clear in your thoughts and ready to learn from anyone. Be it your younger sibling or a junior in school, if he can teach you something, just grasp that knowledge and thank that person.

3. Importance of Experiential Knowledge: Raikva taught his students through his own experiences. He shared with them what he felt. Thus, true knowledge is not simply theoretical but practical. So, when you get a chance to perform any experiential learning activity, put your best. It may be a field trip, an art project or a science experiment, just show your analytical aptitude and understand that it is important that you learn.

To put it briefly, the story of Raikva teaches us the importance of humility, perseverance, kindness and generosity. These are valuable lessons for any student who wishes to pursue knowledge and wisdom.

Reflection Time

Answer the following questions to practically use the teachings in your life.

1. **How many attempts do you make before you give up on a task?**

   (When you have a task at hand, it is your duty to give your best to complete it successfully. The key to success is not giving up at any stage.)

   ____

   ____

   ____

2. **Do you like practical projects and experiments more than theoretical learning?**

   (In today's age it is important to have practical skills and knowledge. You must stay away from the practice of mugging things up. Instead, understand conceptual knowledge by practical application.)

   ____

   ____

   ____

3. **Do you often feel angry and irritated?**

   (Feeling of anger and irritation are common in the teenage phase. To regulate your emotions in a healthy manner, try to meditate.)

4. **How ardently do you believe in selfless sharing, be it things, knowledge or money?** (King Janashruti gave away things but with an eye for fame. But when he met Raikva, he learned the value of selfless service. And so should we learn to do.)

Lesson 8: Giving is Gaining – "Now be prepared for the consequence of this ignorance…" (Chandogya Upanishad)

Story 8: *Brahmachari and the Two Sages*

Here, again we have a story from the Chandogya Upanishad, which relates to a brahmachari and two sages.

Once there was a brahmachari who would meditate on the universal Brahman. This brahmachari was a disciplined student, a great meditator and a seeker who felt that he had practically identified with his deity on account of the depth of his meditation. One day he went about begging for food. He happened to go to the abode of two renowned sages. When he approached them, they were just going to have their meal. He asked them for food, but they did not pay attention to the brahmachari. They turned a deaf ear to this man's pleas. No food was given. They kept quiet as nothing has happened.

Now, observing that he was not being given food and that the great men had simply ignored his very presence, the brahmachari said to them, "O great ones, please listen to what I am saying. There is one great god who swallows up four others. Who is this god? He is the protector of all the worlds. No one beholds the presence of this great god. You two great ones do not realize that all the food of this world belongs to this god, and it is to this god that you have refused food."

The brahmachari was a meditator in an advanced stage. He practically identified himself with the deity on which he meditated. In a way, he had in him the power of the deity. It would not be wrong to say that he could do whatever the deity could do. Now, this deity is the Universal Being, and when the worshipper who had through meditation identified himself with the deity asked for food, it was as if God himself was asking for food.

So, the brahmachari added, "The entire food of all creation belongs to that Deity only, and when it is asking for the food which belongs to it by right, you great men do not give it! So, you understand the consequences of your action. You have done a great offence in ignoring my presence. You do not at all listen to what I am saying. You have not given me the food I asked for and you are keeping quiet as if nothing has happened. Now be prepared for the consequences of this ignorance on your part with regard to this great Deity."

By this the brahmachari meant that he himself was the deity in an embodied form. So, it was a kind of threat he administered to the two persons who were about to take food by themselves without giving it to him who had asked for the same. They would be finished if the deity got angry with them.

After the brahmachari spoke like this, Saunaka, one of the two who were seated there got up. He approached the brahmachari and replied, "You are saying that food has been refused to the great deity, the all-pervading one. Listen to what I have to say on this. You speak like this because you are under the impression that you are a meditator on the universal Brahman and that we know nothing about it. You made a remark that we are ignorant of the presence of this great god to whom all the food belongs. Then what is it that we are meditating on? I will tell you. There is a great Soul, the Self of all beings, the source and essence of all the gods, the creator, the progenitor of all things. He is the one who eats through the mouth of knowledge itself. It is not an ordinary mouth with physical teeth and physical tongue. He has teeth which are shining with the lustre of knowledge. It is the essence of knowledge which is the essence of His being and He swallows all things. He is a great devourer. There is nothing in creation which He cannot devour. Everything is food for him and He consumes it through his own being, not through any external instrument. He is the wisest of all existences. His glory is great indeed. He cannot be eaten or swallowed by anybody, or not even affected in the least by anyone, or contacted and contaminated by any other in any manner whatsoever. But to Him everything is food. He eats non-food too, not only the ordinary food. The eaters themselves are eaten up by Him. This is what we are meditating upon." Having said this, the two sages served food to the brahmachari.

It is believed that the two sages merely wanted to test the brahmachari to find out the depth of his knowledge. They too were learned men and possessed great knowledge, perhaps relatively superior to the brahmachari's own knowledge.

Student Takeaways

The most important lesson from this story is that we learn things for ourselves and not to be arrogant to others. Some takeaways:

1. **Be Free from Pride or Arrogance:** The story teaches us to be humble. No matter how learned you become, you need not be arrogant. You need to show respect towards others. This is applicable in all spheres of life. Whether you are in school, with your parents or friends, speak politely and do not be rude in your behaviour or speech.

2. **Importance of Giving:** The story also teaches us the importance of giving. The two sages offer Brahmachari more than just food; they offer him spiritual guidance and wisdom. This teaches us that true giving is more than just material gifts. It involves sharing our knowledge, time, and resources with others. As a student, if you are able to help your friends in studies, do that. Share knowledge and you will become even more knowledgeable. Teaching others is a way to become more efficient in your skills.

3. **Importance of Learning:** Finally, the story teaches us the importance of being a lifelong learner. Brahmachari keeps himself open to learning from the two sages. So, you should understand that learning is a continuous process, and that you should always be open to new ideas and perspectives. Never think yourself to be better than others, do not be proud, just go ahead and gain knowledge.

4. **Identifying Your Inner Voice:** Deep within us is a voice that differentiates for us between the right and the wrong. And it is that voice that can guide us towards success. But more often than not we fail to listen to that voice. We need to practise listening to our self. And when that begins to happen organically, we can achieve anything we want.

When it comes to self-study, you will find that you might start with a bang to sit and focus for long hours but as time progresses, you start losing your ability to concentrate. That is the time when you need to listen to your inner voice and stick to your commitment. Another aspect of listening to your inner voice is that you develop a sense of intuitive power. It is said that when you study a subject deeply, your mind also needs some freedom to wander a bit. That freedom allows the mind to think from different perspectives and give you some insight into that particular subject you are studying. Albert Einstein is said to have discovered the theory of relativity while playing the violin, and not while sitting in his laboratory. So, when the mind is free and we listen to our inner voice, we develop new dimensions of thinking. Try this method and you will see a major difference when you are doing self-study.

Thus, we get to know the importance of humility, giving and learning. These are all important qualities that students should cultivate in order to become successful and fulfilled individuals.

Reflection Time

Answer the following questions to practically use the teachings in your life.

1. **Describe a time when you were deeply inspired.**

   (It might be an incident or a person that inspired you. You can note it and paste it on desk wall, so as to remind you of things that truly matter.)

   ____

   ____

   ____

2. **What effort do you make to learn outside your classroom?**

   (In today's digital era, it is important to learn from sources other than textbooks. You can learn practical skills from online platforms like YouTube, Udemy etc.)

   ____

   ____

   ____

3. **As an individual, what do you think you can give to others?**

   (Good deeds do not require a lot of sources. Start helping your classmates at school and your parents at home, and you will feel satisfied and happy.)

____

____

____

4. **How patient you are in fulfilling your needs and wants?** (When the brahmachari's wish to have food was ignored by the two sages, he could have burst into anger, but he remained patient and explained his true nature coolly and calmly. How much patience you usually have in such situations?)

____

____

____

Lesson 9: Meditate and Reveal your True Self – "A + U + M + Silence" (Mandukya Upanishad)

Story 9: *The Upanishad of the Frog*

Reading the title 'Upanishad of the frog', you must be wondering, why frog? It may be strange to you but frogs do feature in ancient Vedic Sanskrit texts. In Hinduism, they symbolize transformation and reincarnation. Just think about the lifecycle of a frog; they start as eggs, hatch into tadpoles with gills and a tail, and they lose that tail as they develop into adults with lungs and legs. That is why they are regarded as guardians of transition.

Okay, so the Upanishad 'Mandukya', is named after a frog as the Sanskrit word for frog is Mandukya. The reason behind this is that the text teaches us to leap from the first to the fourth level of consciousness just like a frog and that too by chanting 'Aum'.\

The Mandukya Upanishad is regarded as the Upanishad that explains the real meaning of 'Aum'. The Upanishad says that the entire universe can be explained using the four-factor principle of A + U + M + Silence. It connects with the four-part symbol of AUM as well as the sound of AUM. "Aum" (also spelled "Om" or "Omkar") is a sacred sound and spiritual symbol in Hinduism. The sound of "Aum" is believed to be a powerful vibration that can be used to focus the mind and enter into a meditative state. When it is recited or sung, it is said to produce a positive and calming effect on the mind and body. Many people start and end their meditation and spiritual practices with "Aum". It is believed to be the primordial sound of the universe, representing the beginning, the middle and the end of all things. It is said to embody the three main aspects of the divine: creation, preservation, and destruction, where "A" represents the beginning, or the process of creation, "U" represents the preservation and maintenance of the universe and "M" symbolizes the dissolution and destruction of the universe.

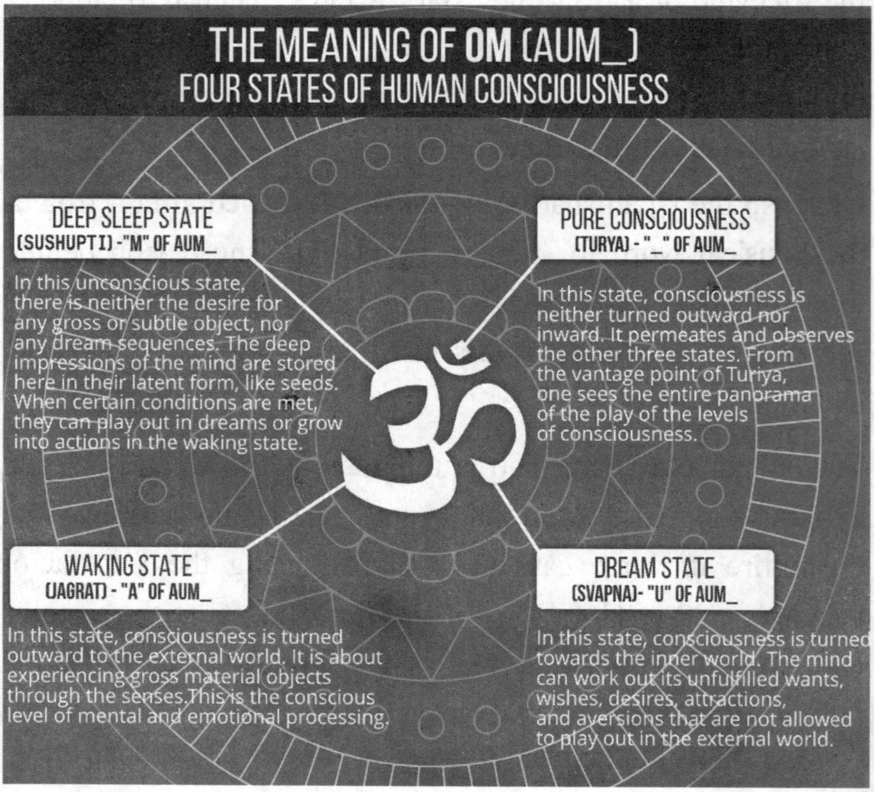

Aum is both a visual symbol and a sacred sound or mantra which we often hear around us. On a piece of clothing, as a tattoo, on jewellery, painting on the wall of a yoga class, we regularly see the Aum symbol (ॐ) at various places. It is a universal representation of yoga and meditation practices. However, many of us do not know how to pronounce it correctly. If it is properly pronounced, it will represent in itself the whole phenomenon of sound production, which no other word can do. Aum is nearest to God, and is indeed the first manifestation of Divine Wisdom. It is truly symbolic of God.

'A' is pronounced as an elongated "Awe". As shared earlier, this sound represents the beginning or the creation of this universe. The sound includes everything within the universe. It is said to symbolise the 'conscious or waking state'. The Hindus associate this sound with Brahma, who is believed to be the creator of this world. The sound originates in the belly, and vibrates in the upper chest. One has to keep the tongue in the lower part of the mouth and part the lips, to create a feeling of openness.

'U' is prolonged as "Oooh" sound. This sound signifies the steadiness that carries a person along and the energy that preserves and sustains him and the world. It is associated with the Hindu God, Vishnu, who is regarded as the preserver. Here, the sound gradually moves forward, rolling along the upper palate and vibrating in the throat.

'M' is pronounced as "Mmmm" sound. This represents the sound of closing in and the beginning of the end and is associated with Shiva, who is often known as the 'destroyer' but also the force of culmination, completion, finalisation.

When forming the sound, we move our tongue to the top of the mouth and bring our lips together to create a protracted humming noise.

After the AUM, there is also a fourth sound, which is silence. It is the infinite pause between one Aum and the next. It has no letter, no sound and no characteristics. It is beyond description and ungraspable, cannot be heard and cannot be spoken of but it contains the entire universe. This is Atman, our true self. This is Brahman.

It is said that Pranava, the sound of creative AUM vibration, is the mother of all sounds. The intelligent cosmic energy of AUM that comes from God is the creator and substance of all matter. Meditation on AUM is the way to realize the true spirit of all creation. AUM is the source of everything. From AUM proceed all sounds. In AUM exists all objects.

The relevance of Aum has always been there and will remain forever. The chanting of Aum can help bring peace and spiritual awareness in our body. We should breathe and inhale before beginning the sound and hold each syllable for as long as possible during the exhale.

As we repeat the mantra, it helps to focus on the vibrations in our body, specifically the vocal chords, chest, and stomach. This resonance has a plethora of physical benefits as well as mental benefits, which includes lowering of blood pressure, relaxing the stomach, calming the mind, harnessing creative energy and bringing spirituality into everyday life.

Coming back to the Mandukya Upanishad, it describes four levels of consciousness as:

1. Jagrata or the Waking State: This is the state of consciousness that we experience when we are awake and aware of the external world. In this state we are fully aware of our body and its functions, and also its free will. The five sense organs (Gyan Indriyas), the five Organs of action (Karma Indriyas) and four internal organs (manas, buddhi, ahankara and Chitta) are all active. We are fully cognisant of all our actions and choices. In this state the physical body is intensely operative and we always think in terms of physical body, physical objects and physical sensations. We are fully awake and all our sense organs and mind are active. We are able to take decisive activities during this stage. The most significant aspect of this state is the capacity of an individual to recognise a thing through vision, taste, smell, sound or feel.

You must be wondering what is this all discussion about Gyan (also written as Jnanya) Indriya and Karma Indriya? Let's see and understand what the Mandukya Upanishad tells us about them. It says that we enjoy, experience and perceive things in nineteen ways in the waking state. According to the Upanishad, consciousness has nineteen mouths through which it eats the food of objective experience. Now, what are these nineteen mouths? They are the five senses of knowledge—seeing, hearing, smelling, tasting and touching. With these five sensations we come in contact with things in the world outside, and enjoy them through our reactions, by means of sensory contact. These five mentioned are called senses of knowledge—**Jnanya Indriyas.** They are so called because they give us some sort of knowledge—either of sight, or sound, or taste, or smell, or touch.

Apart from these five senses of knowledge, there are five organs of action; they do not give us any independent knowledge, but they act. The hand that grasps is one organ of action. The mouth that articulates words is another organ of action. The feet that cause locomotion or movement are also organs of action. The generative organ and the excretory organ also are two of the active elements or organs of action. They act, but they do not give any new knowledge. Whatever idea, knowledge, experience, etc. we may have through any one of these organs of action come through the sensations already mentioned, namely, the Jnana Indriyas. Even when the organs of action act and we are conscious that they are acting, this consciousness is available only through the Jnana Indriyas and not separately though the organs of action, which do not give additional knowledge. It looks as if we have some sensation even through the organs of action, but actually it is not so. The sensation, the experience of the action of the Karma Indriyas as they are called, arises on account of the simultaneous action of the Jnana Indriyas or senses of knowledge. These five senses of knowledge and five organs of action make ten mouths of consciousness.

After this comes the five Pranas—the Prana, or the vital energy in us works in five ways. When we breathe out or exhale, the Prana is acting. When we breathe in, or inhale, the Apana is acting. The Vyana is a third form of the operation of this energy, which causes circulation of blood and creats a sense of liveliness in every part of the body. There is another action of the Prana, which is Udana; it causes the swallowing of food. When we put food in the mouth, it goes inside through the oesophagus and it is pushed down by the action of Udana. It also has other functions to perform. It takes us to deep sleep. Our ego consciousness, our individualised consciousness is pushed into a state of sleep; that also is the work of Udana. Udana has also a third function to perform, namely the separation of the vital body from the physical body at the time of death. Three actions, three performances are attributed to Udana. There is another, fifth one, Samana, which operates through the navel region and causes digestion of food. It creates heat in the stomach and in the naval region so that the gastric juices operate and we feel appetite. Hunger is caused and food is digested by the action of this Samana.

So, there are five Pranas—Prana, Apana, Vyana, Udana, Samana. Five senses of knowledge, five organs of action and five Pranas make fifteen. Besides these, there are four functions of the psychic organ. The internal psyche has four functions designated as Manas, Buddhi, Ahamkara and Chitta. Manas is that part of psyche which registers sense impressions from the external environment. Buddhi or intellect determines, decides and logically comes to a conclusion that something is such-and-such a thing. The third function of psyche is Ahamkara, which is ego, affirmation, assertion, 'I know'. "I know that there is some object in front of me, and I also know that I know. I know that I am existing as this so-and-so." This kind of affirmation attributed to one's own individuality is the work of Ahamkara, known as egoism. The subconscious action, memory, etc., is caused by Chitta. It is the fourth function. So, Manas, Buddhi, Ahamkara, Chitta—these are the four basic functions of the internal organ, the psychological organ.

Thus, we have five senses of knowledge, five organs of action, five Pranas and four operations of the psyche, which comes to a total of nineteen. These are the mouths through which consciousness grasps objects from outside, and we feel secure and happy. All these nineteen things act at the same time in some form or other, with more or less emphasis. Any one of these can act at any time, under special given conditions; and in as much as anyone can act at any time, it is virtually saying that all are acting at the same time. Therefore, it can be said that we are objectively conscious through these nineteen things of individual consciousness acting in the waking condition. We are aware of this vast world of sensory perception and we perceive all objects of the world through these media.

2. Swapna or the Dreaming State: In this state, one is asleep and dreaming. The five sense organs and the five organs of action are inactive in this stage. Only the four internal organs are active. All the impressions gathered through the ten senses are perceived at this state in the mind. The mind is active and thoughts are predominant. Thus, this is the state of consciousness that we experience when we are asleep and dreaming. During this state, our mind creates a world that is not necessarily based on external reality. It is the dreaming stage in which we enjoy the five objects of senses even when all the five sense organs are at rest and only the mind is working. Dreams are the reliving of those experiences from the wakeful stage with some modifications. It is created out of materials supplied from the waking stage. With these experiences unfolding, the individual is denied peaceful sleep, like in a house where though the elders are asleep (the five senses) the naughty child, the mind, is awake and causes illusions. Some believe that the mind weaves dreams because of the experiences that happen during the day and has control over it.

Thus, in this state the physical body is not operating, but the vital, the mental and the intellectual sheaths are active. The Prana is there, the mind is there, the intellect also is there but in a diminished intensity. We breath, we think and we understand in the state of dream. That means Prana, Manas and Buddhi all are active in the state of dream, minus the physical element, namely the body consciousness.

3. **Sushupti or the Deep Sleep State:** This is the state of consciousness that we experience when we are in deep sleep. In this state, our mind is at rest and we are not aware of anything external or internal. Here, we become self-oblivious, unaware as the mind is also at rest along with the five senses. In this state individual is not aware of his worries or reassurances. The individual experiences deluge every night and is in union with the Self and due to ignorance there is no authenticity for the same. In this state of deep sleep, neither the body is operating, nor the mind, nor the intellect, nor is there any consciousness that we are even breathing.

4. Turiya, or the Fourth State: This is the state of pure consciousness that is beyond the three other states. It is often described as a state of complete awareness and transcendence, where the individual self merges with the universal consciousness and experiences ultimate reality and truth. This state is not experienced by the five senses. This state cannot be described and the mind is also unable to comprehend it. This is tied to continuous cycle of births. In this state we experience the sleepless sleep or bliss and become well aware of the union of Self and Absolute. This state is a state of ultimate reality. It can also be understood as "wakeful sleep". This state is beyond the mind and intellect. The consciousness is pure and transcendental. This is the state of 'samadhi'. This state is usually not attained by common man and is only experienced by *yogis* through their 'sadhna'. This is sometimes called the substratum of all the other three states. It is believed that we do not understand the reality in the other three states. When we are ignorant of our true nature, we misidentify ourselves with the body and mind. It is only when we attain Turiya that we know the real nature of the self and the universe.

According to the Mandukya Upanishad, the ultimate goal of human life is to attain this fourth state of consciousness and realize our true nature as pure consciousness. The Mandukya Upanishad claims that the Absolute Reality is attribute less and non-dual. The Upanishad has a unique approach towards Satya or Truth. It provides meditation comprising the word 'AUM'.

The Mandukya Upanishad explains not only who we all really are, but also how, by meditating on the Pranava, we can realize that truth about ourselves. Pranava is another word for 'Aum'. It is said that the whole world, everything that we can see, feel, perceive, intuit, deduce, understand, is that imperishable sound, that cosmic vibration – Aum! It is what has been, what is, what will be, and it is beyond everything, even beyond time, it is Aum! Thus, the Mandukya Upanishad focuses on attuning the mind towards the Ultimate Reality of life through proper meditation.

Another reason for the holy scripture to be named after frog is because the frog generally lives in hibernation for eight to ten months in a year and then comes out in the rainy season for mating. Similarly, it has been said that a perfect man dwells in seclusion during the period of his meditation and comes out in the world only after he has realized the 'Truth' and then spreads his knowledge of Truth to the entire world.

Mandukya Upanishad has come from the Atharva Veda. Among all the other Upanishads, Mandukya Upanishad is the shortest and has only 12 short verses. However, this Upanishad contains within itself the essence of the entire Upanishadic teaching.

Student Takeaways

1. Importance of Meditation: To reach your goals, meditation is a very powerful technique. As a student, it is important for you to set your target and work towards it with dedication and focus. You should develop a regular meditation practice routine to deepen your awareness. Make a habit tracker and track your meditation time. You may start with a very short duration and slowly increase the time. It is an amazing way to increase concentration, relieve stress and perform better.

2. The Concept of Atman: The Upanishad tells us that Atman is not the body, mind or senses, but a pure, eternal, and unchanging consciousness. As a student, this concept helps you to gain a deeper understanding of yourselves and your place in the world. Take for example a situation where you misbehaved with your teacher. The teacher was kind and understanding and did not punish you. However, after that incident, you are not able to face that teacher with confidence. Why does that happen? It happens because of your inner consciousness or atman that tells you that you were not right in your behaviour towards the teacher.

Reflection Time

Answer the following questions in order to practically use the teachings in your life.

1. **What do you think about spirituality?**

   (Spirituality can have different meanings for different people. When any ritual is done in true spirit it becomes SPIRITUAL.) (SPIRITUAL = TRUE SPIRIT + RITUAL)

   ____

   ____

2. **Have you ever tried meditation? If yes, how was your experience?**

   (Visiting a temple can provide you with peace. You must make a habit of going to the temple and sitting in the positive environment for a while to relax your body and soul.)

   ____

   ____

3. **What changes you have observed in your personality as you grew up?** (During metamorphosis, just as a tadpole goes through multiple stages to become a frog, a human being too goes through various stages of transformation in the process of their elevation of consciousness.)

   ____

   ____

Lesson 10: Be One with your Higher Self – "I and the Self" (Mundaka Upanishad)

Story 10: *Two Birds in a Tree*

One important Upanishad is the Mundaka Upanishad, where the word Mundaka, a Sanskrit word, means "shaved" or "shorn," possibly referring to knowledge that shaves away ignorance. The 64 verses of the "Mundaka Upanishad" are composed in the forms of mantras that are used for knowledge and meditation related to learning rather than ritual.

Do you know that our national motto, 'Satyamev Jayate', which means 'Truth Alone Triumphs'has also come from the Mundaka Upanishad? Yes, Pandit Madan Mohan Malaviya is credited with giving the country its motto – 'Satyamev Jayate'. It was Pt. Madan Mohan Malaviya, a great educationist and a national leader of India's freedom struggle, who popularized this term. The mantra originally from the Mundaka Upanishad became the national motto of India after the independence of the country. It was on 26 January 1950, the day India became a republic, that the mantra was adopted as the national motto of India. It is engraved at the foundation of the Lion Capital of Ashoka that is our country's emblem.

This great ancient spiritual text called the Mundaka Upanishad, also has a well-known tale of two birds living on the same tree. The simple story is an allegory for our spiritual journey, the goal and the challenges that we meet along the way.

Once, there were two birds who were bound together in close friendship. They lived on a tree. One lived amongst the lower branches while the other, a dazzling golden bird, perched high up at the top of the tree.

The lower bird was always busy hopping from branch to branch, pecking and eating the fruits of the tree with relish. In trying to find the sweet fruits, it often tasted many sour ones. In contrast to this, the higher bird had no interest in eating any of the fruits of the tree. It always sat silently and kept watching the lower bird.

Once, it so happened that the lower bird tasted a very bitter fruit. Because of this, it shirked away and stopped eating. It looked up and started hopping up the branches towards the higher bird.

Just then, it noticed an especially nice-looking fruit. "What if that fruit is not there tomorrow?" she asked herself. "What if some other bird grabs it?" "What if I never find any other fruit again and, horror of horrors, die of starvation?" Working herself up into a state, she hopped frantically to the new fruit and swallowed it too. The fruit was sweet and tasty! "The higher bird can wait," it thought. So, the bird continued to hop from branch to branch and kept tasting the fruits of the tree.

Whenever the bird was put off by the taste of an unsavoury fruit, it stopped and looked upwards towards the higher bird, admiring its stillness and peace. Then, it started to hop up toward it only to be tempted by yet another luscious, sweet fruit.

One day, the lower bird ate a particularly tart fruit. Totally put off by the taste and tired of chasing after sweet fruits, it became determined to reach the higher bird.

This time, the bird rose up the tree towards the higher bird, staying focussed and carefully avoiding the tempting sweet fruits along the way. Soon, a surprising thing happened; the lower bird began to take on the qualities of the brilliant higher bird. Finally, the lower bird merged with the higher bird.

There it realized that it was never separate from the higher bird as there was really no lower bird. It was all an illusion, like a dream that faded away upon waking up. The lower bird was essentially the radiant and serene higher bird all along.

In true sense, the lower bird is the lesser self, comprised of the senses, the mind, and the intellect. The higher bird is the Supreme Self. Both of them rest in the tree that is the body. But the lower self is too distracted by the luscious fruit, the temptation of the material world, and keeps chasing it, forgetting the friend who accompanied it here, who is even now waiting, patiently, above. Only when she comes across a bitter fruit, i.e., a bitter life experience – does the lower self finally goes in search of the higher one, looking for solace, compassion, and reassurance.

In other words, the ego, the false 'I' and the Self, the real 'I' have an eternal friendship. They live together in the same body, no matter which body they take on. The tree represents the physical body. The ego is in essence the peaceful higher Self. But it has forgotten its true nature and takes itself to be insecure and limited.

The fruits of the tree are actually the fruits of our karma; the results of our own good and bad past actions. Our good past actions reap good karma and bring us happiness in the form of enjoyable experiences, while our bad actions reap bad karma which brings us suffering in life. Our present experiences are therefore based on our past actions. There is no escaping the Law of Karma and we always get what we deserve.

Student Takeaways

As a student, there are several important lessons that can be learned from the Mundaka Upanishad and the tale of two birds living on the same tree:

1. **Understand the Nature of the Self:** The tale of two birds teaches us about the two aspects of the self, the individual self or the ego, and the universal consciousness. As a student, this helps you to develop a deeper understanding of your own identity.

2. **Self-realization:** As a student, you can pursue self-realization. Now, what is this and how would you do that? Self -realization is the process of knowing oneself i.e. the

Atman or the true Self. This can come through practices such as meditation, self-reflection and, if possible, the study of sacred texts. The knowledge of self is the gateway to eternal happiness. So, stay away from emotions like anger, jealousy and hatred and you may feel relieved and stress-free.

3. Developing Spiritual Practices: The story teaches everyone to have self-discipline. As a student, you should be self-disciplined and should be able to integrate this into your daily life. This will definitely deepen your understanding of the self and the universe. You can also become more spiritual simply by staying silent for 5–10 minutes in a day and paying gratitude to God. Be thankful for what you have been blessed with.

4. The Practice of Self-restraint: Self-restraint is the restraint imposed by oneself on one's own actions, and is also known as self-control. The students who demonstrate self-restraint not only succeed and perform well in studies, but also go on to become very successful in life. There is a famous experiment done on students and children to demonstrate how self-restraint helps them succeed. This is called the Stanford marshmallow experiment.

The experiment involves a series of studies on delayed gratification carried out in the late 1960s by psychologist Walter Mischel, a professor at Stanford University. In these studies, a child was offered a choice between one small reward provided immediately and two small rewards if they waited for a short period of about fifteen minutes. During this, the tester left the room and then returned. The reward was something like a chocolate, cookie or a marshmallow. Later, the researchers concluded that those children who were able to wait longer for the preferred rewards tended to have better life outcomes.

The same results will be obtained if self-restraint is exercised while doing self-study. Initially, your mind will wander towards immediate benefits. If you are able to delay your gratifications and focus on studying, you will automatically perform better.

To summarise, the tale of two birds living on the same tree provides some valuable lessons for students, which can help them develop a deeper understanding of their place in the world.

शीलं परम भूषणं

Character is the Best Virtue

Reflection Time

Answer the following questions to practically use the teachings in your life.

1. **Do you practice any spiritual activity?**

   (For about 10 minutes every day, practice meditation. It will not only help you in clearing your mind but also help in aligning your thoughts better.)

   ____

   ____

   ____

2. **Do you keep a journal or a daily planner?**

   (Keeping a planner is helpful to plan and track your daily, monthly and yearly goals. It also works as a constant reminder so that you do not forget things.)

   ____

   ____

   ____

3. **If given a chance, how would you define yourself in a sentence?**

   (Having a self-identity helps you in aligning your ambitions and goals in life. Coming to terms with your identity - your strengths and flaws help you build your self-confidence.)

   ____

   ____

   ____

4. **While choosing any worthwhile goal, you will face lots of distractions. While aiming for fit body, junk food can distract you. While aiming to score high, reels and shorts can distract you. How do you focus yourself on long-term/bigger goals?**

____

____

____

Lesson 11: Know your Atman – "Truth is Prana, so Atman is the Truth of the Pranas" (Brihadaranyaka Upanishad)

Story 11: *The Colloquy of King Ajatshatru and the Proud Balaki*

Now let's learn a little more about the 'Brihadaranyaka Upanishad', which is one of the oldest of the Upanishads. The Upanishad has the central philosophical concepts of Hinduism. It is the largest of the Upanishads, and focuses on the nature of reality and the identity of the Self, or Atman. Here is the story from Brihadaranyaka Upanishad.

Once there lived a learned Brahmin in the land of Bharata. He was called Balaki. He belonged to the family of Garga and therefore, his complete name was Gargya Balaki or simply Gargya. He had travelled through many places and conducted debates at all these places. He considered himself to be the knower of Supreme Truth. He thought he was learned in the knowledge and science of Brahman and was proud of his learning.

He wanted to display his knowledge before an emperor called Ajatashatru, meaning, "someone whose enemy is not yet born". So, during his travel, Balaki, reached the palace of Ajatashatru, the king of Kashi and said, "I shall teach you all about Brahman."

The king was highly pleased and happy that he was getting an opportunity to know more about Brahman, that too from a learned Brahmin. Also, it was an occasion for him to outmatch king Janaka. He received Balaki with all respect and told him, "I am glad you have thought it fit to instruct me. Usually everyone goes to offer such instruction to King Janaka, thinking he is the only one who qualifies to be taught and also because they think he alone is generous with gifts. I too am generous. I shall give you 10000 cows."

King Ajatashatru and learned Balaki sat together and then started the whole discussion.

Balaki started and said, "I meditate upon the person in the sun as Brahman. You also do that meditation."But this was nothing new for the king Ajatashatru. So, he humbly replied, "I do meditate upon the sun, but not as you do. The reason is that the sun is only a conditioned form, and you are considering this conditioned form as the Absolute. This is not the way in which it should be contemplated. There is a Reality behind the sun which is the pre-eminent, the head of all beings, the resplendent. I meditate upon that. This Reality could have taken many forms other than the sun, and so resorting to that Reality behind the form, naturally leads to the realization of every other form. That is what I meditate upon, the King of all beings. One who contemplates thus, in this manner, the Reality behind the sun, becomes supreme among all people. He becomes a king in the circle he moves, and this is the result of such meditation."

The dialogue continued. Balaki, then, referred to the person in the moon as the Brahman and as the object of his meditation. Hearing this, the king replied, "I do meditate upon the moon, but not the way you do. I meditate upon him as the Vast, the White-robed, radiant Soma who covered the whole creation in his immense spread of life-giving Delight. And this excels in its radiance in the measure of the white purity of its forms. One who meditates upon him thus, as the abundant yield of the essence of all life experience, soma, is constant; his sustenance does not decay."

Balaki further pointed to the person in the flash of lightning as Brahman and as the object of his meditation.

But this time also, Ajatashatru could not take it. This was, again, not new to him. He said to Balaki, "I do not meditate upon lightning in the way you have told me. I merely meditate on luminosity. Lightning is one of the forms of potential luminosity. There can be various other forms of Lustre or Brilliance; it can be the lustre of lightning, it may be that of the sun, it may be of the moon, it may be of fire, it may be of one's own understanding. But I contemplate on the Brilliance or the Lustre itself. And I know that one who thus meditates becomes brilliant; his progeny too becomes brilliant."

In this manner the conversation between Balaki and Ajatashatru went on. Balaki continued and pointed out that he meditates upon the person in the sky, in the wind, in fire, in water, in the mirror, in the sound that follows after one as he goes, in the quarters of space, in the shadow, and in the body as Brahman. But every time he was challenged by king Ajatashatru with a fresh explanation of which he had no idea. He realized that there was evidently something more of Brahman which was not covered by the manifestation of which he spoke so proudly. It thus happened that there came a point where Balaki became completely silent. This was because he was left with nothing more to offer.

Ajatashtru took this opportunity and clarified to Balaki that Brahman cannot be known by knowing only that much. There was much more to know about the Brahman. Balaki realized his limitations, and his arrogance melted like an ice cube in the water. He desired to know what he did not know. So, he approached Ajatashatru as a disciple and pleaded with the king to impart to him the right knowledge of the Brahman.

Ajatashatru was a king and a Kshatriya while Balaki was a Brahmin. A Brahmin coming to a Kshatriya as a student was not a usual thing. King Ajatashatru was conscious of his limitation and so hesitated to become a teacher to Brahmin Balaki. But, he did not want to deprive Balaki of the knowledge he wanted to have. So, he took Balaki by hand as a friend and decide to enlighten him on the subject of Brahman. He gave Balaki a very comprehensive knowledge of the Brahman.

He took Balaki for a walk and while walking they came upon a person who was asleep. The king addressed the sleeping person with soft words, but the latter did not wake up. It seemed as if the person was in deep sleep. Then, the king jerked his body and the man woke up. The king asked Balaki, “Where was the jivatman (vijnanamaya purusha) when the person was sound asleep and, where did it come from when he was jerked?”

Balaki had no answer. He could not understand the king’s words. Then the king explained that when the person was asleep, his jivatman was taken away along with the consciousness of all the vital organs, which was resting in the sky of the heart.

The king told Balaki that all lokas, all the gods, all the bhutas come out of the atman when it is conscious. This is the truth of truths. Truth is prana, so atman is the Truth of the pranas.

Student Takeaways

As a student, here are a few things that you can learn from this story:

1. **Never Feel Proud:** Balaki, the teacher in this story, was very proud of his knowledge and expertise. He was of the belief that he knew everything. This pride resulted in his downfall, as he found it difficult to learn from Ajatashatru. Similarly, as a student, you should never feel proud in what you know. Be humble and a keen learner all through your life. Arrogance usually results in failure at some point of time.

2. **Be Humble:** In contrast to Balaki, Ajatashatru was humble and open to learning. He was willing to listen to Balaki's teachings, but along with this, he did not hesitate to question his assumptions and looked forward to expanding his knowledge. This humble behaviour allowed him to grow and learn, while Balaki remained stuck to his limited perspective. Thus, being humble is the greatest asset of any student. Without humility, there can be no humanity. Thus, as shared earlier, always be ready to learn things and do ask questions politely.

3. **Critical Thinking:** Ajatashatru's ability to think critically and question Balaki's teachings was a key factor in his success. By asking thoughtful questions and challenging assumptions, he was able to gain a deeper understanding of the world and expand his knowledge. Therefore, it is good for a student to think and then grasp things. If you want to be thorough with a topic, do not believe in mugging up the concept. Instead, think about it and ask whatever doubts come to your mind. This

will help you develop your critical thinking. Ability to think critically and creatively in any situation is the key to success in life.

4. Be Persistent: Ajatashatru's persistence in seeking knowledge and challenging assumptions is another important lesson for students. Learning is a lifelong process, and it requires dedication and hard work. So, be persistent and work towards your goal. For example, if you want to learn graphic designing, simply knowing how the software tools work won't make you an expert. You have to be persistent in your approach and practice designing every day, no matter how busy you are.

Thus, the story of Ajatashatru and the proud Balaki teaches us to be humble and persistent. Along with this, we should always be open to learning and practice critical thinking.

Reflection Time

Answer the following questions to practically use the teachings in your life.

1. Do you also feel proud when you accomplish something great, for example winning an award at school?

(Feeling joyous after getting an award is natural for everyone, but if it is accompanied by a feeling of superiority over others, it might be pride. You must be careful not to take excessive pride in an accomplishment but rather strive for better results each time.)

____

____

____

2. How often do you ask questions in class?

(Asking questions in the class improves your retention and helps in concept clarity. You can set a daily goal of asking 2-3 questions every day. In order to ask questions you must study on your own.)

____

____

____

3. Do you have any hobby that you pursue regularly?

(Hobbies make you feel good. They fill your day with happiness. Be it sports, music, art or a simple every day walk, a hobby refreshes you and fills you with energy. You must remember that a hobby is not something that you are excellent at doing but it is something that you fully enjoy.)

____

____

____

Part II: Connect the Dots-The Influence of the Ancient on the Modern

1. Seeking Inspiration in the Most Unlikely Ways

Indians find it very difficult to appreciate their country, its history, its heritage, its achievements and its knowledge. We simply fail to praise the wisdom that our sages had. We are not able to recognize and value all that our country has given to us.

The basis for all scientific discoveries and inventions is to explore, observe, experiment and interpret. For this, one needs to bank on prior knowledge, facts that are documented, so that the results lead to new or improved status in the given realm. It is in this context that Vedas, which are the primary texts of Hinduism, assume great importance.

Most of the modern discoveries have been referred to in the Vedas and these are not mere literal concepts but proofs are available for their existence.

We often hear that nothing is new, everything has come from Vedas but we do not accept that and always question - Was there any science during the Vedic age? The answer to this question is a big 'Yes'. The Vedas have scientific descriptions of all aspects of human life, right from sociology to cosmology. However, the Vedas primarily emphasize the science of consciousness. According to the Vedic theory, it is only through the evolution of consciousness that human beings can find true happiness and satisfaction.

The ancient Vedas, which seem to be a thing of past, have always been connected with many of the present-day inventions.

Science has always been an integral part of the Vedas. It may be surprising but the Vedas hold a very important place in this modern era. In today's stressful, fast-paced life, they are still relevant. In fact, many of the modern-day inventions, discoveries and theories have been found to be a part of the Vedic age. Many scientists who have studied Vedic literature to gain a thorough understanding of scientific, spiritual, psychological, and behavioural knowledge have proved this. Thus, in India, science and spirituality have always been together.

The Vedas contain data related to all fields of science. The Vedas are believed to have deep connection with various branches of Science, Mathematics, Psychology, Economics and Environment. In fact, Vedas have inspired several western scientist in developing important scientific theories and concepts besides also influencing other fields of study like laws, mathematical modelling, medicinal studies, astrology, cosmology, metallurgy and life science. It has been proved that many modern-day inventions are somewhat related to discoveries that took place in Vedic age thousands of years ago. Many temples, buildings and monuments are influenced by Vedic tradition. All the scientific discoveries and inventions that have been inspired by the Vedas are listed below. Read about some important facts from the Vedic times, understand their connect with our modern age and you may definitely feel a sense of pride.

1.1 Architecture in Vedas

The Vedas, being ancient Hindu scriptures, do not specifically focus on architectural principles or designs. However, they do mention various aspects related to architecture indirectly, primarily in the form of ritualistic instructions and descriptions of sacred spaces. Do you know that the Madurai Meenakshi Amman Temple has a thousand pillar hall but there is absolutely zero echo. Is this not enough to gauge the knowledge of our ancestors about concepts of architecture? Here are a few key points regarding architecture as found in the Vedas:

- **Yajna (Vedic Ritual):** The Vedas contain detailed instructions for performing yajnas, which are complex rituals involving the construction of fire altars and sacrificial structures. These rituals often required the construction of elaborate temporary structures, including altars, platforms, and sacrificial pits.
- **Vastu Shastra:** Although the systematic treatises on Vastu Shastra (the traditional Hindu system of architecture) came into existence at a later period, the Vedas do touch upon certain principles that align with Vastu concepts. For example, they emphasize the orientation of buildings and the proper placement of various elements within a space.
- **Mandala:** The concept of mandala, which refers to the arrangement of spaces within a geometric pattern, is mentioned in the Vedas. Mandala patterns are associated with the construction of fire altars, where precise measurements and geometric designs were employed.
- **Sacred Spaces:** The Vedas describe the importance of sacred spaces and the selection of appropriate locations for performing rituals. The selection of a site for constructing temples or other religious structures was considered

crucial, taking into account factors such as proximity to water bodies, mountains, and auspicious sources of energy.

- **Symbolism and Cosmology:** The Vedas often use symbolic language and metaphors to describe cosmic and divine principles. These symbolic representations extend to the construction of sacred spaces, where the arrangement of elements, such as pillars, gates, and chambers, may represent cosmic principles and deities.

These days, Vastu Shastra is popular across the world. The reason behind this is the universal need for peace and harmony. It is believed that the application of the principles of Vastu Shastra in home construction and design brings along good health, wealth and happiness in life. In the present era, a lot has been discussed and written about it. People are demanding the designs of their houses and buildings as per the principles and guidelines of the Vastu Shastra.

Vastu Shastra finds its origin in the Athrava Veda. During the Vedic period, the Indian *rishis* and *munis* performed the rituals according to the geometry of the Solar System. They had complete knowledge of planets, stars, etc. even before Copernicus came up with his groundbreaking theory. They were definitely the scientists of the Vedic era.

The science of Vastu Shastra deals with the layout and direction of building architecture. Though it is traceable to at least the year 3000 BC in the Vedas, it is a hot current topic across the world today. The Gumbaz found on the mosques all over the world actually originated as the interlocking dome in the Stupa of the Buddhist architectural tradition in India. The temple architecture found all over India speaks volumes for the design concept related to engineering. The building of huge structures without the use of any modem equipments actually tells the story of an advanced feat in construction practices.

Vaastu Shastra is an ancient science that deals with the study of designing spaces in an interpersonal relationship with the forces of nature and cosmic energy. Directions and orientations play a very important role. Since we live in a world full of latest technologies, modern infrastructure and high-rise buildings, following the principles of ancient times is not possible. However, if we understand the logic, we can apply it in simple ways without compromising on aesthetics.

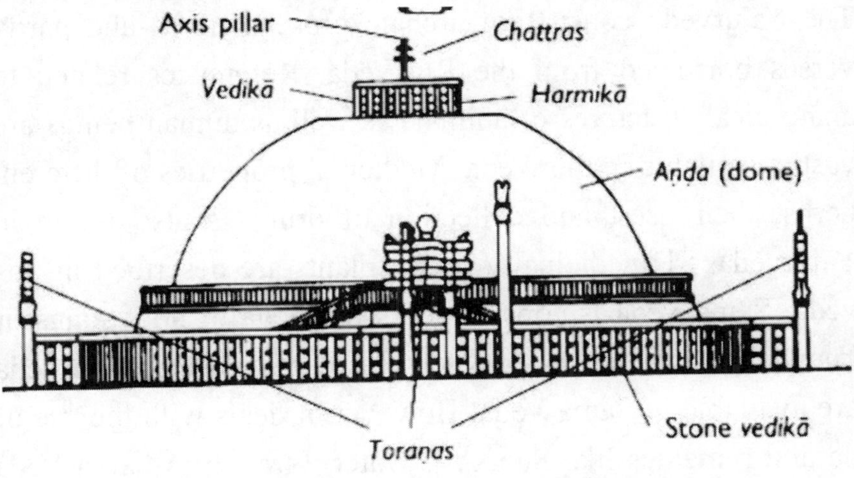

1.2 Science of Health and Medicine from Vedas

The science of Dentistry and Medicine in India has a profound history which can be traced to the Vedas and hence the origin is considered as divine. According to historians, there is evidence of dentistry being practiced way back in Vedic times. One archaeological site even showed evidence of healers curing tooth disorders with bow drills. Our modern dentists also make use of similar tools. There is mention of many drugs, predominantly of plant origin, prevention of diseases and maintenance of health in the Vedas, mainly in the text books of Ayurveda. The origin of ancient dentistry or the Danta Sasthra in India is synonymous with that of Ayurveda. Lord Brahma, the creator of the universe is considered to be the creator of Ayurveda and hence that of ancient dentistry. Rig Veda discusses 67 plants and also the use of natural remedies. It also talks about exposure to sun rays, which our allopathic doctors also recommend these days, the good old source of Vitamin D.

The Yajurveda consists of archaic prose mantras and partly verses borrowed from the Rig-Veda. References related to anatomical structures of animals as well as human beings are vastly available in this Veda. Medicinal properties of different herbs, their uses, and collection of drugs is also found in Yajurveda. 81 medicinally useful plants are described in this veda. Sama Veda is considered as the Veda of holy songs or knowledge of melodies. Only few references related to Ayurveda are available in Sama Veda. However, it deals with the use of natural remedies like Sun, Air, Water, Fire etc. Atharva Veda contains detailed description of various aspects of Ayurvedic concepts, anatomical structures of human body, digestion and metabolism, blood circulation, diseases and their causative factors, preventive measures and treatment with herbs.

Plastic surgery, a major part of medical sciences, is popular all over the world. Countries like America and Brazil have been arguing over which place is the world's plastic surgery capital. However, plastic surgery was first formulated by Sushruta, also known as the "father of Indian medicine" and the "father of surgery". This is because he wrote the earliest works on surgery and medicine in the world. That is why it is widely believed that modern science and technology owes a lot to Indian knowledge system.

Sushruta's famous book 'Sushruta Samhita,' which is considered as one of the oldest texts, vividly deals with several methods of performing plastic surgery. This text is a part of the Atharva veda. Sushruta was considered a great healer and a sage and people believed that his power in medicine was gifted by God to him. The Sushruta Samhita recorded all about how a physician practices the art of surgery and follows all the procedures which include performing plastic surgery and the removal of cataracts.

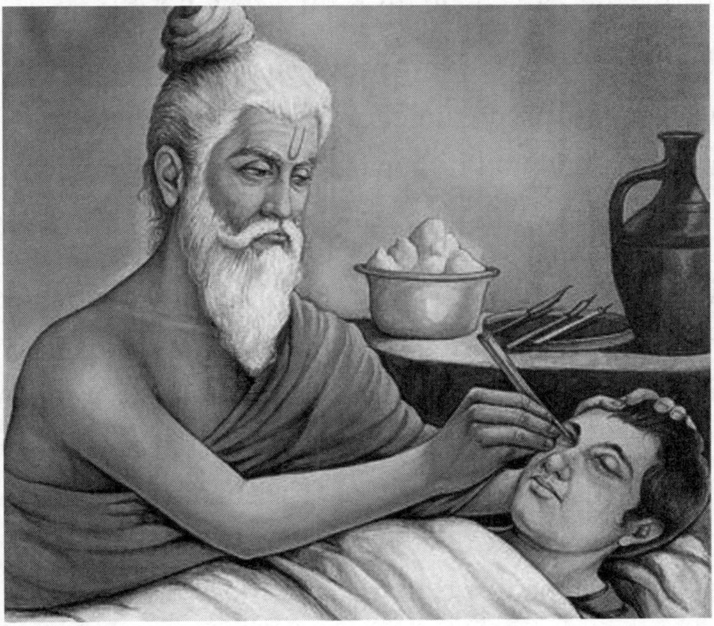

Yes, you read it right, it is surprising but the cataract surgery was known to the Indian physician Sushruta. In India, cataract surgery was performed with a special tool called the *Jabamukhi Salaka*, a curved needle used to loosen the lens and push the cataract out of the field of vision. The eye would later be soaked with warm butter and then bandaged. Greek philosophers and scientists came to India where these surgeries were performed by physicians, and introduced this practice to the western world.

Another surgery, Rhinoplasty, also known as the 'nose job,' which is usually done either to improve the breathing function of the nose or to improve the cosmetic look of the nose, has also come from Sushruta. His text provides the first written record of a forehead flap rhinoplasty, a technique still used today to reconstruct a nose. He used a flap of skin from the forehead, called a pedicle, to form a new nose.

Besides these general surgeries, Sushruta also gave an in-depth account of the treatment of six types of dislocation. This continues to spellbind orthopaedic surgeons even today.

1.3 Ayurveda: The Alternate Medicine

Ayurveda, which has its roots in the Vedic literature, has inspired places like Switzerland, where it is recognized as an alternate medicine for many years now. In 2010, the World Health Organization (WHO) published the benchmarks for professional training in Ayurveda. The content is taken from the syllabus for Ayurvedic doctors in India. Ayurveda is recognised as a system of medicine in 16 countries including Hungary,

Switzerland, Cuba and Brazil. The other countries are Nepal, Sri Lanka, Pakistan, Bangladesh, UAE, Oman, Saudi Arabia, Bahrain, Malaysia. The ayurveda products are being exported to more than 100 foreign countries either as medicine or food supplement. It is amazing that its acceptance is fast increasing globally. Recently, during the Covid period, the herbs and remedies mentioned in Ayurveda caught the attention of the entire world. People used all kinds of ayurvedic remedies to build better immunity and stay away from this dangerous infection.

Ayurveda is a branch of Atharvaveda, the fourth book of Vedic literature. Ayurveda blends our modern lifestyle and health-oriented habits with the ancient wisdom of using natural substances, medicines and herbs to enable us enjoy a healthy and happy life. It provides ways to keep us stress-free and disease-free. The basic aim of Ayurveda is to restore the individual balance between mind, body and spirit. Ayurveda is the Upaveda (sub veda) of Atharva Veda. The word Ayurveda is made of two words - Ayu and Veda. The word Ayu doesn't mean just life, but the union of Shareera (body), Indriya (sense organs), Satva (mind) and Atma (soul). Veda, as you know, means knowledge. Hence, Ayurveda means the knowledge of the union of body, sense organs, mind and soul. Ayurveda Shastra aims at keeping a person healthy and managing or curing diseases (mind, body or both) that manifest in that person.

In today's scenario where problems like arthritis, obesity, hypertension, heart disease, nervous disorder, colds, colitis, constipation, obesity, skin problem and ulcer have become common problems, ayurvedic medicines are widely used to treat several such physical as well as psychological conditions. Ayurveda has the ability to treat many chronic diseases such as cancer, diabetes, arthritis, and asthma, which are untreatable in modern medicine. Ayurvedic treatment is non-toxic and non-invasive. Also, this can be safely done along with conventional medicines. Ayurvedic medicine aims at maintaining and restoring body's own capability to have balance and fight with ailments. Because these medicines are composed of natural ingredients, they do not have any side effects. These medicines make the person's body and mind disease free. Functions of lungs, spinal cord and existence of other internal organs, including nervous system, were also discovered by the ancient Indians.

To talk about Ayurveda without the mention of AYUSH would not be appropriate. The word AYUSH stands for Ayurveda, Yoga, Naturopathy, Unani, Siddha and Homeopathy. It refers to the Ministry of Ayush, which was formed with a vision to revive the profound knowledge of traditional Indian systems of medicine. The Ayush ministry works towards promoting homoeopathy and ayurvedic medicine in India. Though Ayurveda, yoga and homoeopathy are an integral part of Indian culture, they are often given less weightage than modern medicine. The AYUSH ministry works towards decreasing this discrimination. The goal of AYUSH is to reduce diseases and improve people's mental, physical and spiritual health.

We are sure that this wonderful information about Ayurveda would definitely make you feel proud as an Indian.

1.4 Food from the Vedas

These days health issues like hypertension, diabetes, thyroid, arthritis and many such names have become quite common. You may find every second person suffering from any of these ailments. However, it was not so in the Vedic age. So, where have we gone wrong? The reason behind this is irregular, unhealthy eating habits and lack of exercise. Now, after Covid experience, people have slowly started moving towards Vedic food habits. You must have often come across seminars and workshops being held on Vedic food in the last few years. Such events are evident of the popularity that Vedic food has started getting.

There is a significant amount of food knowledge contained in Rig and Yajur Veda. These Vedic texts throw considerable light on the food and drinking habits of the people. It is apparent that people of that age ate food rich in various macronutrients. There is also mention of the best usage of lubricant (ghee and oil) for the body. Ghee is essentially a form of clarified butter and is termed as superfood. It facilitates healthy digestion, decreases inflammation, reduces the risk of cancer and other diseases and much more. It is good for high-heat cooking because the lack of milk solids makes sure that it doesn't burn.

The Vedas also talk about the importance of cookware. The goodness of cooking in the earthenware was highlighted as food prepared in these vessels retains its natural flavour. The heat is also evenly spread and maintained. Copper pot also has very good medicinal properties as no bacteria can survive in it. Iron pans are rich in minerals and food cooked is tasty. The food cooked in silver vessels cools down the body, relaxes and rejuvenates it. Food cooked in copper and brass vessels help in increasing the immunity level and metabolism. Betel leaves also help in controlling the imbalances of the body. It is also believed that fruits are better than juices. As per the Vedic food science, it is strongly advised to eat water-rich vegetables and fruits like melon, watermelon, grapefruit, radish etc as it keeps the body temperature balanced, less frequent urination which means the body need not retain temperature etc.

The Vedas mention six tastes or rasas namely astringent, bitter, pungent, salty, sour and sweet. Vedic cooking recommends incorporating each taste in every meal keeping the constitution of your body in mind. A balance in these six tastes help to achieve balanced nutrition and good health.

The importance of spices like cumin, turmeric, pepper cannot be ignored. The benefits of using turmeric in daily cooking have always been highlighted. It cleans the water, is antifungal, anti-bacterial and good for immunity. That is the reason why the recovery rate of Indians is usually faster as compared to people elsewhere.

The Rigveda and the hymns of Yajurveda mention about the use and importance of different types of spices like pepper, fenugreek, coriander, cardamom, ginger and mustard. Atharvaveda remarks about the use of turmeric for treating jaundice and leprosy. Ayurveda describes the use of spices and their importance with various medicinal properties. The epics *Ramayana* and *Mahabharata* also mention about spices used on various occasions.

In the classic book *Susruth Samhitha*, the renowned surgeon, Susrutha, refers to the use of spices in surgery. In a book by famous ancient Indian philosopher, Vatsayana, there is a detailed mention of various spices.

Many spices, used in India for ages, have secured a safe place in the international domain. In the recent times, many global companies have taken the patent for these spices owing to their benefits on a physical and mental level. The use of spices like

Ginger, Tulsi, Neem, Turmeric and Garlic has become quite popular these days. So, just go for these and use them as much as possible.

1.5 Yoga in Vedas

Taking time out for oneself is a luxury in the modern world for most of us. It has become very difficult to balance family, work and take out some time for oneself. Usually, this desire remains unfulfilled. Stress caused by worries often leads to a plethora of diseases which affect the mind and the body. This has led to the modern human seeking to flush out toxins and achieve peace and self-healing.

Because of all this, Yoga, an ancient discipline was reborn and popularised in the modern world. Yoga originated in ancient India around five thousand years ago. The Rig Veda is the earliest known source of its documentation. Yoga comprises physical, mental and spiritual practices and promotes self-healing. The word 'Yoga' means to unite. It is a merger of mind, body and soul. An ancient practice that originated in India, it has become popular worldwide as a form of exercise and stress relief.

Yoga is a way of living. If incorporated in daily life, it does wonders to the human body and mind. It works on physical, mental, emotional, social and spiritual levels of human beings. It helps in improving the quality of life. It provides guidance on how to think, behave and grow to become a fully mature person. Yoga brings harmony between body and mind. It is an art and science for healthy living.

These days children face too much stress. Be it school, home, playground, etc. This leads to many problems such as physical, mental and emotional. When these health hazards create problems for long, they lead to diseases. All these problems originate due to imbalance in our physical, mental and spiritual levels. They are closely related to materialistic way of life; endless ambition is the primary cause of our suffering. According to the Upanishads, yoga is a higher state of consciousness and a process to ease the mind and manifest the wisdom. Children who practice yoga regularly experience improved concentration, reduced blood pressure, and better grades in the academics, improved interpersonal relationships, more confidence and better sleep. Thus, this ancient practice is a boon for today's generation.

Our honourable Prime Minister Narendra Modi has an important role in making yoga popular. He was the one who proposed to celebrate International Yoga Day during his speech to the UN General Assembly in 2014. As the United Nations approved the same, June 21 is now observed as the International Yoga Day since 2015. While Yoga has always been India's own way to emphasizes on fitness, it was PM Modi who was responsible for its worldwide recognition and spreading awareness about its importance across the world. Yoga became a massive source of well-being in the COVID-19 pandemic. As moving outside was restricted, numerous people started practising Yoga to stay fit. The Narendra Modi-led government kept promoting Yoga and its benefits even during the COVID days.

1.6 Astronomy in Vedas

Ancient Indians were skilled astronomers, and their knowledge of the stars and planets is reflected in the Vedas. Many modern inventions, such as telescopes and satellites, have their roots in ancient astronomy. According to the Rig Veda, the year was divided into 12 months of 30 days with the total number of days in each year being 360. To ensure that the years averaged 366 days, two periods were added every five years to bring the calendar back in line with the solar year. So close to what modern astronomers say today. It is true that the major modern inventions in the field of science and technology are reflections of Vedic knowledge. They speak of the facts that were already mentioned in the Vedas over thousand years back. The modern replicas of scientific theories are in sync with explanations in the Vedic scriptures.

Though modern science credits Copernicus for proposing our solar system, it was the Rig Veda that first noted the central placement of the Sun and other planets orbiting it in the solar system. In Vedic literature, there are many references to planetary movements. Rig Veda describes the movements of Earth and other planets around the Sun. Along with this, there are other references that describe the motion of other planets around their own axes while moving around Earth. At the same time they rotate around Sun in fixed positions relative to each other.

The Hindu cosmological time cycles gave the time taken by Earth to revolve around the Sun as 365.2563627 days. This is just 1.4 seconds longer than the modern value of 365.256363004 days given by the scientists, isn't this surprising!

Ancient astronomy cannot be complete without the mention of Surya Siddhanta, the oldest book known to man on Astronomy. It is the first among the traditions or doctrines in astronomy of the Vedic era. In fact, it is the oldest ever book in world which describes earth as sphere but not flat, gravity being reason for objects falling on earth etc.

The Surya Siddhanta is an invaluable resource for anyone interested in understanding the movements of celestial bodies, including the sun, moon, and planets. It also provides intricate details about eclipses and the phases of the moon, making it an essential read for astronomers and astrology enthusiasts alike. The text also has a wealth of mathematical calculations that enable the precise determination of the positions of celestial bodies at any given time. Perhaps one of the most noteworthy contributions of the Surya Siddhanta is its accurate calculation of the length of a tropical year. This refers to the amount of time it takes for the Earth to complete one orbit around the sun.

The text is not limited to Earth, but also states the motion, and diameters of the planets. For example, it states the diameter of Mercury as 3,008 miles, an error of less than 1% from the currently accepted diameter of 3,032 miles. It also estimates the diameter of Saturn as 73,882 miles, which again has an error of less than 1% from the currently accepted diameter of 74,580.

The Surya Siddhanta also contains the roots of Trigonometry. It used sine, cosine and inverse sine for the first time! It also contains the earliest use of the tangent and secant.

1.7 Vedic Science in Hanuman Chalisa

There are millions of devotees of Hanumanji in India and abroad. Hanuman Chalisa is a very popular prayer among them. Written by Goswami Tulasidas, a great devotee of Lord Rama, the prayer glorifies Shri Hanumanji. But do you know that this prayer also has a bit of science? It is believed that in one of these verses of Hanuman Chalisa, Tulasidas had given an accurate calculation of the distance between the Sun and Earth. According to the calculation presented in Hanuman Chalisa, distance between Sun and Earth = 12000 x 1000 yojanas = 96 million miles = 153.6 million kms, which is very much close to modern calculations given by the modern scientists. This information definitely sounds amazing. It is astonishing that Tulsidas mentioned the distance to this level of accuracy as early as in 16th century when the Western astronomers, with the help of telescope, were still trying to figure out the distance.

This also means that people of Vedic period knew the size of the celestial bodies and the distance between them. According to Vedic **Astronomy**, the distances to both moon and sun are about 108 times their diameters. Incidentally, this is one of the reasons why the number 108 is considered holy in Hinduism.

1.8 Atomic Theory from Vedas

The discovery of atomic theory is credited to John Dalton, an English chemist, physicist, and meteorologist.

However, do you know that Kanad, an ancient Indian sage, scientist and philosopher propounded a theory of atoms to explain the creation and existence of the universe. Our ancient sages first conceptualized the idea that matter consists of indivisible units and cannot be further divided into smaller particles. The smallest particle, i.e. atom infuses the entire universe. It cannot be destroyed and retains its original form under all situations. Sage Kanad was the first to give clear picture about this concept. While Kanad lived during 600 BC, Dalton belonged to the late 18th and 19th century. Kanad was the founder of Vaisheshika, one of the six major schools of Vedic philosophy from ancient India. This text explained the creation and existence of the universe by proposing an atomistic theory. The great sage applied logic and realism to draw conclusions.

1.9 Management Principles in Vedas

Management has become a part and parcel of everyday life. Be it home, office, factory, society or any other place management principles come into play through their various facets like management of time, resources, personnel, materials, machinery, finance, planning, priorities, policies and practice. **Management techniques** were also prevalent in the ancient times. All our ancient scriptures like Ramayana, Mahabharata, and the Upanishads, have great discussions on management strategies.

The modern management concepts like vision, leadership, motivation, excellence in work, achieving goals, meaning of work, attitude towards work, nature of individual, decision making, planning etc., are all discussed in the Vedas.

1.10 Mathematical Principles in Vedas

It would not be wrong to say that **Mathematics** is the most important aspect in sciences. Ancient mathematics or Ganita included arithmetic, algebra, astrology, geometry and astronomy. As per the Chinese records, many books written during the 9th and 10th centuries, such as Brahmagupta's Sidhanta, Charaka Samhita, and Susrata Samhita were translated into Arabic. Later, they were translated from Arabic to many other languages including German.The concept of zero was first discovered in ancient India and is believed to have been first used in the Vedas, particularly in the work of mathematician Aryabhata. Today, zero is an essential component of mathematics and computing.

Also, Vedas offered significant help in the field of practical geometry in the construction of altars for grand sacrifices at king's court. The concepts of acute angle, obtuse angle, right angle etc. were apply in the construction of fire altars.

Binary numbers have also come from the Vedas. Binary is the basic language in which computer programs are written. Binary basically refers to a set of two numbers, 1 and 0, the combinations of which are called bits and bytes. The binary number system was first described by the Vedic scholar Pingala, in his book Chandahśāstra.

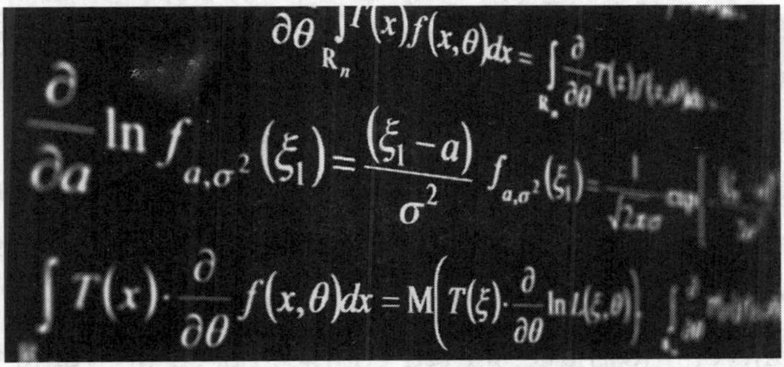

Vedic mathematics has become quite popular since the last few years. However, it is pleasing to know that it is an ancient scheme based on 16 formulas (sutras). These are easy and simple methods for fast mental calculations. Many researchers have worked on it for its usefulness in various branches like engineering and astronomy. It helps in faster and accurate mental calculations. By using Vedic mathematics, one can solve any difficult equation in addition, division, multiplication, algebra, trigonometry, square, square root, cube, cube root only by mental calculations. It offers solutions to complex mathematical problems that are simple and easy to follow.

It states the concept that the diagonal chord of the rectangle makes both the squares that the horizontal and vertical sides make separately. In Vedic mathematics, a decimal system of tens, hundreds, and thousands etc. where the remainder from one column of numbers is carried over to the next has been developed. The advantage of this system of nine number signs and a zero is that it allows for calculations to be made easily. Further, it has been said that the introduction of zero in India as a definite part of number system is one of the most important contribution and development in mathematical sciences.

In today's fast-growing era where competitive exams have become a ladder to achieve success, Vedic maths helps in faster mental calculations, thus reducing time to solve difficult mathematical equations. It also helps to reduce mathematical anxiety among students and regain interest in maths, with purpose of making mathematics easier. Today, many universities have started courses based on Vedic maths, yoga & Vedic literature. Our Prime Minister Shri Narendra Modiji has also taken keen interest in Vedic formulas and is making efforts to make it popular across the globe.

The great Indian mathematician Bhaskaracharya who preceded Newton by five hundred years made some discoveries concerning the principles of differential calculus. He also produced treatise on both plane and spherical geometry and algebra and the treatise contained remarkable solutions to problems not known in Europe till late seventeenth century. The binary code which is the very backbone of any software computer application, the algorithm and the WWW fundamentally rest on the concept of zero, which is found in Vedic literature.

1.11 Space and Military Related Concepts in the Vedas

The word Dhanu means weapons in general and the pair of bow and arrow in particular. Hence 'Dhanurveda' means military science or the arts of archery. Another name commonly used is 'Dhanurvidya', which is exclusively concerned with archery. Dhanurveda is a Upveda which mentions the use of bows and arrows. In other words, Dhanurveda is another name for Indian military science.

Vedas explain in great detail the organization of armed forces i.e. the military of the times. Well-defined rules have been laid out regarding armaments and warfare. Many modern day missiles and weapons have their early reference in Vedic literature. It is really amazing that, conceptually, the rules and arts are comparable to modern times.

These are just a few examples of Vedic science and its connection with the present-day technology. In today's scenario, where stress and depression have taken a prime seat, it is our duty to combine the knowledge of Vedas and the talent of modern scientists for the betterment of our society and environment. We need to work more closely towards better human life in terms of physical, mental and social health. At the same time, we need to preserve our environment for our future generations. It may be better for countries to work together and not in isolation to make this earth a better place. We should work for the welfare of the whole world using scientific methods coupled with ancient Indian wisdom.

Vedic principle is to explore higher levels of truth in an unbiased manner and be honest to the results of this exploration. Science and Vedas go hand in hand. Thus, the approach of Vedas is way different from the rest of the religious output. It is great that Vedas do not spoon-feed. They don't expect you to find truths of nature and world by memorizing certain verses. In contrast to this, Vedas urge humans to put efforts, conduct experiments, reflect upon those experiments and discover wisdom by making best use of life. Vedas are definitely a trusted guide, coach and mentor.

Coming to any new scientific discovery, if it is harming the environment or other countries, it should not take place. However, if it is done in accordance with India's Vedic culture and it helps to enhance the use of natural resources, keeping in mind environment's safety, it should certainly be done.

Today, at a global level, there are many challenges that are making our life difficult. A recent example is that of the Covid-19 pandemic that shook our world from its roots. Not to forget that even in such a situation, it was Indian herbs and spices that helped people in building immunity. Global experts acknowledged the worth of Indian ancient knowledge and this itself is an achievement of Ayurveda, which is a part of the Vedas.

We have many such bigger challenges on global warming and other environmental, social and economic fronts which can be positively worked out and solved if taken the help of Indian Vedic philosophy. It is important for world leaders to realize the importance of India's deep knowledge and work together for the betterment of our planet. Our Vedic knowledge about science definitely has the potential to bring harmony among nations. There can be positive growth and development for all. We all should make a combined effort to bring out the best for everyone around us.

The Vedic civilization has given the world a wealth of knowledge and wisdom that still holds relevance today. While there may not be a direct connection between modern inventions and the Vedic texts, certain concepts and ideas found in the Vedas have influenced or inspired modern inventions.

Inventions and discoveries as mentioned in ancient Indian texts have led scientists and researchers around the world to make some breakthrough innovations. What can be termed as an era of the technological history of India, fields like architecture, astronomy, metallurgy, logic, mathematics, metrology and mineralogy and their subsequent branches were pursued by Indian scholars.

2. On the Path of Implementing Knowledge

Having gained knowledge about Vedas, we now understand that though the Vedic civilization is age-old, it is still a rich powerhouse of wisdom. Today, when we are facing stress from many factors - emotionally abusive relationships, harassment and trolling, financial instability, politics and even social media, Vedas provide us solutions to lead a peaceful and stress-free life. Over indulgence in social and digital platforms have impacted our relationships just like the ever-increasing amount of screen time that has resulted in a serious social media hangover. With so many things around us, it is our mental health that has been hit badly. It is time for us to consider the importance of Vedic knowledge and use it to improve the quality of our lives. We need to accept that the way of life that we, as a society, have become accustomed to needs to be changed.

Our Vedas offer us a comprehensive and complete approach to happiness and health. They emphasize the importance of balancing the mind, body, and spirit to achieve overall well-being. As a mindful student belonging to today's age, we should practice some Vedic ways to unlock happiness and health and strike a balance between our mind and body. Here are some tips:

2.1 Yoga: Yoga is an ancient practice that originated in India during the Vedic times. Nowadays, it is practiced worldwide. It involves a series of physical postures (asanas) and breathing exercises (pranayama) that help to balance the body and mind. Practicing yoga regularly can help to reduce stress, increase flexibility, and improve overall health. Yoga can also help to increase mindfulness, promote relaxation, and enhance self-awareness. Through regular practice, yoga can become a way of life that promotes physical, mental, and spiritual well-being. To summarise, yoga facilitates the mind-body-soul connection.

2.2 Sitting for Long periods: Do take a break and stand or move around while you work or study. Sitting for long hours continuously may not be good for your health. It may lead to heart disease, diabetes, and a shortened lifespan.

2.3 Meditation: Meditation is another important Vedic practice that can help to calm the mind and promote inner peace. There are many different forms of meditation, however the basic idea is to focus attention on a single object, such as your breath or a mantra. Regular meditation can help to reduce stress, improve concentration, and promote a sense of well-being. It can also help to increase self-awareness and mindfulness, which can lead to a greater sense of peace and happiness. It just takes a few minutes a day to meditate but its benefits are enormous.

2.4 Ayurveda: Ayurveda is an ancient system of medicine that emphasizes the practice of herbal remedies, massage therapy, and dietary changes that are tailored to an individual's unique constitution. Ayurveda can help to balance the body and mind, promoting overall health and well-being. Ayurvedic practices can also help to prevent disease and treat a variety of health issues. These days more and more people are getting attracted towards this alternate system of healing.

2.5 Mindful Eating: According to the Vedas, food is not just a source of nourishment for the body, but also for the mind and soul. Eating mindfully, with awareness and gratitude, can help to promote good digestion, reduce stress, and foster a deeper connection with the natural world. Mindful eating involves paying attention to the taste, texture, and aroma of your food, as well as the physical sensations that arise during eating. By eating mindfully, you can improve your connection with food and promote overall health and well-being.

2.6 Add More Veggies and Fruits to Your Diet: Eating lots of vegetables and fruits can help prevent chronic diseases, so eat more of these and keep the junk food aside or maybe, have it once-in-a while.

2.7 Self-Care: The Vedas emphasize the importance of self-care and self-love as essential components of overall health and happiness. Taking time out for yourself, whether it be reading a good book, leisurely taking a walk or any similar activity, can help reduce stress and promote a sense of well-being. Self-care also involves taking care of your physical health, such as getting enough sleep, exercising regularly, and eating a healthy diet. By prioritizing self-care, you can promote overall happiness and well-being.

2.8 Follow Your Passion: Life has become too busy nowadays but you need to set aside some time each day to make yourself happy. Many of us work so hard every day that we simply forget how great it feels to enjoy painting, dancing, music, writing, gardening or swimming.

2.9 Show Gratitude: Take some time each day to be thankful for all that you have - family, friends, pets, food, shelter, health, or the beauty of nature.

2.10 Laugh Often: Believe in the quote - **Laughter is the best medicine**. Do not take life too seriously. Relax and enjoy the good times.

Thus, the Vedas offer a holistic approach to happiness and health. By incorporating Vedic practices into our daily life, we can achieve greater happiness, balance, and overall well-being. It's important to remember that each individual is unique and may require different approaches to achieve balance and well-being, so it is important to listen to our body and find what works best for us. With consistent practice and patience, we can unlock greater happiness and health, and strike a balance between our mind and body.

The Vedas help us become aware of our true nature. The knowledge that Vedas have is old because it was received directly from the Universal Consciousness by the sages. However, it is amazing as it aids in distinguishing between what is right and wrong, true and false etc. Giving a human form to principles and ideas, such as Indra, Agni or Varuna, makes us relate to them and inculcate those principles in our daily lives. The main aim of the Vedas is to help us find a balance in different aspects of our lives in order to reach higher spiritual goals.

Ending - What next?

Let's connect!

Thank you for reading this book. I hope you enjoyed it! If you are interested, there is a lot more going on behind the scenes!

Follow my Instagram page **@avinash_studycoach** where I share daily motivation and study tips for students to score higher marks in exams.

You can also follow my Youtube Channel, Avinash Agarwal, where I share many inspirational stories for students.

You can also subscribe to my free and paid online courses where I provide guidance on parenting and tips to students for success in competitive exams. You can also find more details about my courses on **avinashagarwal.in**

For weekly dose of motivation through unique stories, you can also subscribe to my Newsletter at **avinashagarwal.in/newsletter**

If you want to organize webinar for your school/coaching/club/organization please write to me at **avinash@aiets.co.in**